SALES FORECASTING:

A NEW APPROACH

Books:

Building to Customer Demand, by Tom Wallace and Bob Stahl

Sales & Operations Planning, 2nd Edition, by Tom Wallace

Sales Forecasting: A New Approach, by Tom Wallace and Bob Stahl

Master Scheduling in the 21st Century, by Tom Wallace and Bob Stahl

ERP: Making It Happen, by Tom Wallace and Mike Kremzar

The Instant Access Guide to World Class Manufacturing, by Tom Wallace (editor)

Customer Driven Strategy, by Tom Wallace

The Innovation Edge, by Bill Barnard and Tom Wallace

High Performance Purchasing, by John Schorr and Tom Wallace

MRP II: Making It Happen 2nd Edition, by Tom Wallace

Videos:

Sales & Operations Planning: A Visual Introduction, by Tom Wallace

Procurement in the New World of Manufacturing, by Bob Stahl

SALES FORECASTING: A NEW APPROACH

Why and How to:

Emphasize Teamwork, Not Formulas

Forecast Less, Not More

Focus on Process Improvement,
Not Forecast Accuracy

Thomas F. Wallace
&
Robert A. Stahl

T. F. Wallace & Company
2002

First Printing: January, 2002
Second Printing: February, 2002, Minor revisions
Third Printing: September 2002, Conversion to QuarkXPress (Windows)
Fourth Printing: August 2003, Addition of Appendix H, minor terminology change and
                  other minor revisions
Fourth Printing: July 2004, minor terminology change and other minor revisions
Fifth Printing: September 2004, minor changes to Sales & Operations Planning section
Sixth Printing: Additions to Appendix C

International Standard Book Number (ISBN): 0-9674884-1-9

Printed in the United States of America

This title and other books and videos by Tom Wallace and/or Bob Stahl may be ordered on line from: www.tfwallace.com
                                                T. F. Wallace & Company
                                                513-281-0500

Also available from the APICS bookstore: www.apics.org
                                                800-444-2742

Bob Stahl may be contacted at: RStahlSr@aol.com
                                                R. A. Stahl Company
                                                508-226-0477

TABLE OF CONTENTS

List of Figures

Dedication

During the writing of this book, America was attacked. We, like all Americans, were shocked, stunned, and angered by this unspeakable sneak attack. We were also thrilled by the heroism displayed by so many people during these events.

Therefore, we dedicate this book to all those who lost their lives in this action — the most notable of whom are the New York firefighters and police who entered the World Trade Center bravely and willingly in an attempt to help their fellow citizens, and the heroic passengers on United flight 93, whose bravery and vigorous action prevented another mass murder.

This book is written primarily for people in manufacturing enterprises. Most of those who died worked in the financial world; others were with the Department of Defense; the City of New York, and the airlines. However, they were our fellow citizens — our sisters and brothers — and we salute them.

May their sacrifice not be in vain.

Acknowledgments

Thanks also go to the talented and highly experienced professionals who reviewed this book and gave invaluable feedback:

Tom Asacker
Author and Speaker

Cathy Budd
Global Supply Chain Manager
The Dow Chemical Company

Jennifer Clark
Director of Product Development
Candle-lite Inc.

Dick Crawford
Executive VP/General Manager
B. A. Ballou, Inc.

Chris Gray
President
Gray Research

Tom Kilgore
North American Central Demand Planning Manager
The Procter & Gamble Company

Arvil Sexton
Former VP, Manufacturing Resource Planning
Drexel Heritage Furnishings, Inc.

Pete Skurla
Principal
Oliver Wight Americas

Steve Souza
Principal
Oliver Wight Americas

Fred Thorne
Principal
The Supply Chain Partnership

Lee Wallace
Support Services Manager
Caelus, Inc.

Don Weintritt
Global Supply Chain Director
The Dow Chemical Company

Rick Wright
Director, Sales & Operations Planning
Senco, Inc.

Thanks, folks. You made it a lot better.

David Mill (cover design), Kim Nir (copyedit), and Kathryn Wallace (electronic typesetting) did the kind of superb job that we've grown accustomed to. It's a delight to work with true professionals, and we thank you.

Bob Stahl offers a big "thanks a million" to his wife Pat. Bob's very grateful for the support, the patience, and the encouragement she has provided, both during this project and throughout his career.

Last and certainly not least, a special word of appreciation goes to Chris Gray, mentioned above, for his work on this book that was valuable, extensive, and above and beyond the call. Thank you, sir.

Foreword

Some years ago a colleague of ours, Ollie Wight, was teaching a public seminar. An early part of the session was devoted to self-introductions by the attendees. Here's what happened when a marketing vice president introduced himself:

Marketing VP: *"Hi. I'm Joe Smith. I'm the VP of Marketing with Ajax Widgets."*

Ollie Wight: *"I'm not familiar with the widget business. Who's your competition?"*

Marketing VP: *"Manufacturing."*

At the time we thought it was humorous. But we've encountered this kind of situation too many times to think it's just a funny story. It's too widespread.

Jim Burlingame, formerly Executive Vice President at the Twin Disc company in Racine, WI, claimed "Ninety-five percent of all marketing-manufacturing relationships are adversarial." Jim's number may not have been accurate to four decimal places; maybe the percentage is 88 or 98.6. But Jim's point was right on the mark: The "national average" is that people on the commercial side of the business — Marketing and Sales — normally do not have warm, friendly, supportive relationships with the folks in Operations — Manufacturing, Purchasing, Materials, Logistics. And vice versa.

Why is this so? Why do these people hassle each other instead of devoting their time and mental energies to serving the customers? Well, there's a lot of reasons: functional silo organizations, misaligned performance measurements, left-brain vs. right-brain personalities, unenlightened leadership that pits one group against another, and — oh yes — not doing the forecasting job well. This includes lack of accountability, poor forecasting processes, dealing with too much detail, and unclear objectives.

This last issue — not doing the forecasting job well — is what this book aims to fix. We hope it helps companies make things better on the forecasting front. Doing a better job of forecasting can help the individual company increase its customer service (order fill), reduce inventories, run the plants better, and — last but certainly not least — sell more product. But there are implications far beyond that.

First, we believe that the New Economy does exist. Things are different today. We can have good growth, high employment, and low inflation all at the same time. And while we haven't completely eliminated the business cycle (yet), we have dampened its ups and downs by more than a little bit. Better business processes — Total Quality, Sales & Operations Planning, Lean Manufacturing, Enterprise Resource Planning, Just-in-Time, and others — have contributed enormously to this.

Second, better sales forecasting processes can help not only the individual firm, they also can have a beneficial effect on the economy as a whole as they take hold widely throughout industry. As a large number of manufacturing enterprises get better and better at forecasting, the New Economy will work even better, productivity will continue to increase, inventories will lean out even more, and the business cycle will be dampened further.

There are three themes that play throughout this book. You've seen them already; they're on the front cover:

Emphasize Teamwork, Not Formulas

Forecast Less, Not More

Focus on Process Improvement, Not Forecast Accuracy

We'll have more — a lot more — to say about each of these in the pages that follow. We hope it's helpful for you, for your company, and for your country.

Tom Wallace,
Cincinnati, OH
513-281-0500
tomwallace@fuse.net

Bob Stahl
Attleboro, MA
508-226-0477
RStahlSr@aol.com

January 2002

How to Use This Book

Time is money, and typically we don't have enough of either. Not everybody will need to (much less want to) read all of this book. So here are some thoughts as to who might read which chapters, in order to learn what they need to know and still make efficient use of their time.

Anyone who will be directly involved in the sales forecasting process should read the entire book, as should those charged with the installation and maintenance of the forecasting software.

Members of the Executive Team should read at least Chapters 1 through 3, 8, and 9. Ditto for others in the company who will not be "hands-on" with forecasting but have an interest in it.

Chapter 1

NEED

Gripe: *You can't forecast this business.*

Stop! Before you read this book, let's make sure it'll be helpful. After all, it's going to take some of your time to read it, and you'll probably have to expend some mental energy to do so. If the book won't help, that's not a good investment of those resources.

This book will probably be helpful if you:

1. are the president, chief executive, or general manager of a business that makes products and you see a major gulf between your Sales & Marketing folks and those in Operations.

2. work in Sales & Marketing, and continually get beat up for bad forecasts.

3. work in Operations and feel that the sales forecasts you get are really awful.

4. are a field salesperson who just doesn't understand why you need to go through this agony called forecasting.

5. believe that, with better forecasts, your company could do a better job of shipping customer orders quickly, complete, and on time.

6. believe that, with better forecasts, your company could do a much better job of anticipating financial surprises.

7. are considering buying new forecasting software.

On the other hand, this book won't be highly helpful if your current forecasting processes are very good, or if you work in a high-tech company where a large percentage of your forecasting challenge is with new products and end-of-life issues with existing products. Nor will it help you if you're convinced that the key to forecasting excellence lies in advanced statistics and superior forecasting software — or if you work in non-manufacturing industries such as banking, retailing, insurance, or the airlines.

Gripes About Forecasting

Here's a group of people we'd like you to meet, along with some of their favorite comments about forecasting. These folks, incidentally, are all employees of the World Wide Widget Works.

Sam Mason, VP Sales & Marketing: *"You can't forecast this business."*

Len Davis, Director of Logistics and Materials: *"If only we could get an accurate forecast, it would solve most of our problems."*

Paula Morgan, Product Line Manager: *"How does Len know the forecasts aren't accurate? I doubt if he's looked at one in years. I think he ought to concentrate on eliminating all these backorders instead of griping about our forecasts. Besides, forecasting's not in my job description; I'm staying out of that game."*

Paul Shaw, Production Scheduler: *"We need more detail in our forecasts."*

Irene Schmidt, Director of Information Services: *"Our forecasting software gives us everything we need."*

Vic O'Connor, VP Operations: *"The forecasts are awful. It's no wonder we have trouble shipping on time. But I'm not optimistic that it'll get better. We start lots of stuff around here, but don't finish much. Why should better forecasting be any different?"*

Carol Fox, CFO: *"We're happy with our forecasting; we've been doing it this way for over ten years."*

Fran Adams, Forecast Analyst: *"Making forecasts is a waste of time around here; nobody ever reads them, especially Operations. And now, that dingbat Paul Shaw in Scheduling wants us to give him even more detail. Hello?!"*

Dave Palermo, Division President: *"When I was in Sales, I used to say that we know the forecasts are going to be wrong, so why bother with them? But now something tells me that better forecasting might help."*

Don't be misled by their words. This is a good bunch of people: They're hardworking and successful. They love to make their customers happy and to give their competitors fits. But . . . they do seem to have a problem with this forecasting stuff. They're not working well together. Words like divisive, contentious, and adversarial come to mind.

Why Bother with Forecasting?

Well, if this forecasting stuff causes us to be unhappy with each other, maybe we should just skip it. So, first let's address one of the president's comments: "The forecasts are going to be wrong, so why bother?" Maybe he's right. Maybe his company, or some others, might not need to go through this forecasting agony. After all, it is time consuming. It doesn't directly add value to the product. And, oh yeah, it's going to be wrong. Here are some characteristics of a company that might be able to get by without forecasting:

- Their customer order fulfillment times are longer than their total procurement and production lead time. In other words, after they get the customers' orders, they can buy the material, make the product, and ship it — and that timing is just fine with the customers. And . . .

- They can add or reduce capacity very quickly and economically. They can turn on a dime — increasing or decreasing their output — and they can do this for virtually no cost and with no negative impact on people's lives. And . . .

- The owners of the business do not require forward financial planning. This can happen when the company's stock is closely held and not publicly traded.

Is your company like this? No? Then you might want to keep reading because just about every other kind of company needs to forecast. Here are three reasons why.

1. Ship Quick

Almost every company has to ship customer orders quicker than the cumulative lead time[1] for its products. For products that we call "make-to-stock," this is a way of life; they must complete the product and put it into finished goods inventory before the customer orders arrive. For make-to-order companies, this means that material must be bought and frequently production must begin prior to the customer order.

Now some of you might be thinking: Wait a minute. We have that situation but we don't do any forecasting. Our response: oh yes you do. Someone, somewhere within your company is forecasting (and we'll bet that the word "forecasting" is not in their job description). Sometimes these "forecasters" are in Purchasing. They need to commit for purchased materials far ahead of customer order receipt. They are predicting (forecasting) future needs for purchased items. Typically these predictions are based heavily or totally on past history.

---

[1] This refers to the total time required to procure the material and produce the product.

Other folks who forecast (even though it's not in their job description) work in areas like Production Planning and Scheduling. Frequently they need to commit jobs into production prior to customer order receipt, and they do this based on some kind of a prediction — a forecast — also usually based on past history.

Let's raise several questions: One, are these the best people to do the forecasting and, two, is past history always the best basis for the forecast? Answers: no and no. Stay tuned for the reasons why.

2. Change Capacity

In some companies, increasing or decreasing capacity can be difficult and costly. In other companies, it's less so. But very few manufacturing organizations can sharply change their output rates with no cost or effort. For most companies to change capacity cost-effectively with no negative impact on product quality, advanced planning and very controlled implementation are required. What enables this to happen is forecasting sufficiently far into the future.

How far is "sufficiently?" Well, it depends. If a capacity increase will involve mainly people rather than equipment and will require more than merely overtime, the labor market can be a key factor. If the jobs call for low skills with little training, and if there are people looking for jobs, the forecast would need to go out a number of weeks or months into the future. This is necessary to cover the lead time needed to hire and train new people. On the other hand, if the labor market is tight, and if the jobs are highly skilled with long training times, the forecast may need to be in quarters or years — perhaps the same as capital equipment.

On the flip side — a decrease in capacity and hence, workforce — one might feel that not as much advance notice would be needed. All that needs be done is to have a layoff, right? Again, if it's a tight labor market, looking farther forward may be very desirable in order to avoid a layoff that's followed shortly by a rehire. Also, if the decrease could be planned in advance, might it be possible to reduce the workforce via attrition and thus avoid a large layoff, which is typically difficult and disruptive to the people affected and their families, and costly to the company?

If new equipment is involved in a capacity change, then a longer forecast horizon is normally required — often quarters or years. Here also, the "heads-up" that can come from a good forecasting process can be invaluable, giving engineering and manufacturing people the time to do a proper job of developing specifications, getting quotes, evaluating alternatives, and making the right selection.

3. Financial Planning

If your company is publicly traded, you are required to do financial planning: projecting income, expenses, profits, investments, cash flow, asset levels, and so on. Even if your company is not publicly traded, you need to do a good job of financial planning in order to run the business responsibly.

Well, financial planning is all about the future. As such, it requires a forecast. And, invariably, that forecast is forthcoming — even from the folks who say: "You can't forecast this business." They may grumble, but they do the forecasting. Why is this?

We think there are several reasons, one being that the annual budgeting cycle is so deeply ingrained in most companies' business processes that people simply accept the fact that it has to be done. Another is that the forecasts used in the budgeting process are most often in dollars — and dollars tend to be easier to forecast than units. Third, the CFO in most companies has lots of clout; he or she can make the forecast happen.

A summary of the different uses for forecasts is shown in Figure 1-1.

Figure 1-1

USES FOR FORECASTS

Use	Unit of Measure	Forecast Horizon
Financial planning	Dollars	Current and future fiscal years
Sales planning	Units/dollars	Weeks, months, quarters
Capacity planning	Units/hours	Months, quarters, years
Advanced procurement	Units	Weeks, months, quarters
Master scheduling	Units	Weeks, months

Too Much Forecasting?

It's true that many companies don't forecast enough. However, your friendly authors believe that many companies forecast too much. Too much detail, too far out into the future. For example, there is some sentiment within the World Wide Widgets operations group for forecasts 12 months into the future by individual end item[2]. The question to ask is "why." Are you going to release production orders into the plant 12 months ahead of time? If the production lead time is three weeks, why do you need 12 months of end item detail in the forecast?

Operations might respond by saying they need that much forward visibility for long-range procurement. Our response here would be, "Okay. We're not quarreling with the need for a 12-month or longer horizon. But why do you need end item detail? Within a given product family — medium widgets, for example — there are materials and components common to all products in that family, and others that are unique to only some products. Might it not be better to forecast overall volume for the medium widget family (covering the common components) and then use percentages to reflect the unique items?"

We believe this is the way to go, and in Chapter 5 we'll get into the details of how to construct and use planning bills of materials — and thereby not have to wade through enormous amounts of detail. Forecasting is work; it consumes time and brain power. Let's not do any more of it than is necessary to get the job done[3].

Now for a couple of definitions.

Volume Forecast: A forecast by product grouping such as families, classes, and so forth. Also called the aggregate forecast or the product group forecast, it is used for sales planning, for capacity planning at the plants and suppliers, and for financial analysis and projections.

Mix Forecast: A forecast by individual product. Sometimes called the detailed forecast. It is used for short-term scheduling for plants and suppliers, (and may be required for certain long lead time, unique purchased items).

---

[2] Sometimes referred to as a "stockkeeping unit." (SKU). A more rigorous use of SKU is that it includes location: An end item at a given location is an SKU.

[3] One company we know with good statistical forecasting software will let the detailed, mix forecast run out into the future for a year or more. They spend virtually no time on the details out beyond the Planning Time Fence, but rather use the detail to aggregate up to the volume level. We think that's okay; the issue is how one spends one's time. We'll have more to say on this in Chapters 3 and 6.

Please check Figure 1-2, which depicts the relationship of volume versus mix forecasts. Please note that the mix forecast goes out only to a point called the Planning Time Fence. This is the point in the future inside of which detailed planning and scheduling must be present, and typically is based on the cumulative lead time for manufacturing and purchasing. (For a more complete explanation of the Planning Time Fence, please see Appendix A.)

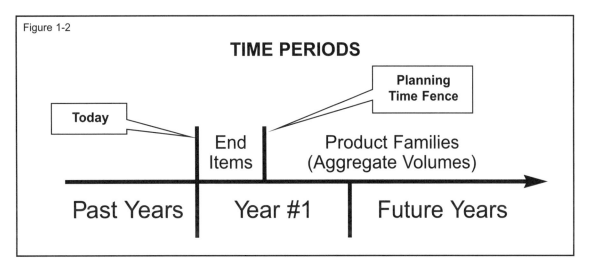

Figure 1-2

TIME PERIODS

One Set of Numbers

During the time period when both the volume forecast and the mix forecast exist, i.e., inside the Planning Time Fence, they *must* agree. The sum of the detailed mix forecast must equal the aggregate volume forecast. This is one example of operating with one set of forecast numbers.

The reverse — operating with more than one set of numbers — can happen in companies where Sales is a totally different organization from Marketing. Sales makes a sales forecast and so does Marketing. The problem is, they don't agree. So which forecast should Operations use? We don't know.

We've also seen companies where some Finance & Accounting folks do sales forecasting, typically as part of the annual budgeting and financial planning cycle. And, of course, the odds are quite high that this forecast doesn't agree with the others. So which forecast should Operations use? We don't know.

We do know what the company should do: Get rid of the multiple forecasts, assign accountability for forecasting, and insist on only one set of numbers with which to run the business. Once the forecast is agreed upon, once it becomes what some people call the consensus forecast, then all parties must use it. It's no longer legitimate to get the forecast and then "apply judgement" to it, i.e., make it something different.

Oh my goodness, we've used the "a" word: accountability. Yes, there does need to be accountability for this important forecasting activity, and we'll get into that in the next chapter.

Gripes and Tips

Let's return to the item with which we began this chapter, the gripe. It said: "You can't forecast this business." We'll see a number of these gripes — negative comments about forecasting — throughout the book, and we'll try to respond to them with tips and often by citing various principles of forecasting. Here's the first:

> **Principle #1: Sales forecasting is being done in virtually every company that produces and sells products, either formally or by default. The challenge is to do it well, better than the competition.**

You not only can forecast the business; you must. You have no choice. So if you have to do it, why not do it very well, better than the competition?

If you need more encouragement, please take a look at our next principle, which we hinted at in the Introduction:

> **Principle #2: Better forecasts enable companies to give higher customer service (order fill), to lower the inventories, to run the plants better, to work more cooperatively with suppliers, and — last but certainly not least — *to sell more product.***

A listing of all the forecasting principles identified in this book is contained in Chapter 9.

Chapter 2

ACCOUNTABILITY

Gripe: *Forecasting's not in my job description;*
my job is to sell product.

Some years ago, a major U.S. corporation had a seemingly robust strategic planning process. They had a large centralized planning staff at the corporate office, and these people would develop the strategic plans for the various divisions. These plans would then be "handed off" to the operating divisions to be executed. This process looked great on paper and was well respected by financial analysts, investors, and other people outside the company.

The Accountability Principle

You might be surprised to learn that the company doesn't do it that way any more. Why? Because it didn't work. Why didn't it work? Well, for a variety of reasons, perhaps the most important being that this approach violates a key principle dealing with account-ability: *The people who develop the plan should be the same ones who execute it.*

Imagine a conversation among that company's CEO, the corporate director of strategic planning, and the president of a division that had failed to accomplish the plan.

CEO: *Bill, your division didn't make plan. Why not?*

Division President: *The plan was unrealistic. There was no way that plan was attainable. We told 'em that.*

Corporate Planner: *We believe the plan was attainable. If the division had just got on with doing it, instead of complaining about how hard it is, they would have gotten it done. We very carefully explained to them how to do it.*

Division President: *Most of the guys on your staff have never worked in an operating division. They don't have a good handle on what happens in the real world.*

And on and on. Things like ownership, accountability, and buy-in are pretty hard to come by in this situation.

The accountability principle, which couples planning with execution, also applies to forecasting. The people who develop the forecast — the demand plan — need to be the same ones who will execute it. So what does this say about who does the forecasting? Should it be the buyers? No, because they don't execute the sales forecast. They don't sell stuff; they buy. How about Paul Shaw, the production scheduler? No, for pretty much the same reason — he doesn't sell, he schedules. Anne Meyers in Accounting? She doesn't sell either; she keeps track of the money — but once a year at budget time she gets in the forecasting business, by default.

When filtered through the prism of the accountability principle, the answer to the question, "Who owns the forecast?" becomes clear. *It has to be Sales & Marketing.* They are the people who sell the product. They execute the plan. They're the company's experts on the demand side of the business. Thus the principle here is that Sales & Marketing people own the sales forecast; they are accountable for its development, authorization, and execution.

Let's look at a few examples of companies with different organizational formats and see how this principle can be applied.

Case 1: a combined Sales & Marketing group reporting to a senior executive in charge of both the Sales and Marketing functions. This is straightforward. What needs to come from this group is one set of forecast numbers authorized and approved by that senior Sales & Marketing executive.

Case 2: separate Sales and Marketing departments, each one headed up by an executive who reports directly to the president[1]. In this case, it's incumbent on these two executives to do whatever it takes to reconcile the differences, if any, in their separate forecasts, and to come up with one set of forecast numbers. This is an important responsibility. They owe one set of forecast numbers to their colleagues in Operations and Finance, and also to their boss, the president. We'll have more to say on this in Chapter 6.

---

[1] Throughout this book, we'll use the term "president" to refer to that executive who has overall bottom-line responsibility for the business unit. As such, this person would typically have all of the major business functions reporting in to him or her: Sales & Marketing, Operations, Finance & Accounting, Human Resources, and Research & Development. Other terms for president include chief operating officer, general manager, managing director, business unit leader, or — in a smaller corporation — chief executive officer.

Case 3: more than one Sales & Marketing unit, reporting directly to the president. One might see an organization with, for example, a Retail Business Unit (selling primarily to mass merchandisers), a Contractor Business Unit (selling to contractors) and a Professional Business Unit (selling to architects and engineers). This can get particularly tricky when different business units are *selling the same products (SKUs)*.

One company we're familiar with had this arrangement. They wanted to create the position of forecast analyst, i.e., someone to operate their statistical forecasting system and pull the forecasts from the different business units together into one set of numbers. The problem they faced: where organizationally to locate the new job. There were three Sales & Marketing departments (reporting to the president) but they needed only one forecast analyst. They were reluctant to chop up the forecast analyst job into three part-time positions, due to the level of expertise and training required to operate their forecasting software[2].

They decided to locate the forecast analyst within Materials Management, which was a part of Operations. If they had done this and no more, we're confident that it wouldn't have worked. But, very wisely, they went a step further: The president made it very clear that *forecasting responsibility was with the business units* (retailer, contractor, professional). Forecasting was part of their jobs and they were accountable. The forecast analyst served in a supporting role to the business unit directors and product managers.

Thus the forecast analyst was not accountable for the forecast itself. Rather, she was held accountable for making it as easy as possible for the business unit people and the field sales force to come up with rational, reasoned forecasts.

Inclusion

In all of the three cases above, the goal should be to develop forecasts that represent the best thinking from all of the important players. Are the field sales folks important? Absolutely. They're on the front lines, dealing with customers every day. Their knowledge of their customers' status, plans, and future direction is vital to the forecasting process in most companies, particularly in the short run.

Are customer service people — the ones who talk to customers and take their orders — important for forecasting? In many companies, their input is important and needs to be reflected in the forecast. Here too, they often are most helpful in the near term.

---

[2] This particular company had selected forecasting software that was quite complex, perhaps unnecessarily so. Simpler software might have given them more flexibility with this organizational issue.

Are the product management people — the marketers — important to the forecast? You bet. They know the future plans and directions for their products: pricing, promotion, advertising, and other things that will impact the future level of sales.

How about Fran Adams, the forecast analyst at World Wide Widgets? Is she important? Yes, very. But let's not make her too important. Let's not make the mistake of thinking that she does the forecasting and that the forecast numbers are hers. A job like Fran's involves communicating with lots of people, getting their input, crunching numbers, and presenting the results to Sales & Marketing management for their review, modification, and acceptance. She puts the numbers together; she knows those numbers very well; she "eats, drinks, and breathes" those numbers every day; but the numbers are not hers. They belong to the people in line jobs in Sales & Marketing.

Gripes and Tips

Here's the gripe from the start of this chapter: *"Forecasting's not in my job description; my job is to sell product."* And our response is that the forecast is the company's expression of anticipated demand from customers. It is not a statement of supply (Operations' responsibility) or revenue (Finance's responsibility), although both of these functions are impacted by the forecast. Thus:

> **Principle #3: Sales & Marketing people own the sales forecast; they are accountable for its development, authorization, and execution.**

One action that might flow from this principle is to check the job descriptions of the Sales & Marketing people. Do they specify sales forecasting as one of the requirements of the job? If not, should they? We believe so, because only when this accountability issue is crystal clear will the company's forecasting processes work well.

Right now, some of you Sales & Marketing folks might be thinking: "Okay, I guess forecasting is necessary, and I can't argue with the idea that it's our job. But how are we going to do a good job of it when everybody agrees that the forecast won't be accurate?"

Our reply: Who said anything about the forecast having to be accurate? We sure haven't — nor will we. Stay tuned.

CHAPTER 3

PROCESS

Gripe: *It's impossible to make any sense
out of this forecasting stuff.*

One of the steps in improving forecasting is to demystify it. Forecasting should be viewed as no different from many of the other things people do within a company: It's a process, but not a physical process such as building a product, or packing and shipping it. It's an informational and decision-making process.

We've learned from Total Quality Management that processes can be improved and that's almost always a good thing to do. The reason: *better processes yield better results.* And, we hasten to add, *better forecasting processes yield better forecasts.*

Do you have problems with your forecasts? Most companies do. Do people in most companies, when they realize that they have problems, roll up their sleeves and go to work improving the forecasting process? Not in our experience. Usually they gripe, whine, complain, and point fingers. That, assuredly, does not improve the forecasts. In fact, it may make them worse.

Forecasting as a Process

Processes have inputs, a conversion phase, and outputs. Let's take the case of making a product. In Figure 3-1, we see a simplified schematic showing that raw materials are input to a conversion step that transforms the materials into finished product.

Figure 3-1

THE PRODUCTION PROCESS

RAW MATERIALS ⟶ CONVERSION ⟶ FINISHED PRODUCTS

Well, forecasting happens the same way. There are 1) inputs, usually from a variety of sources, 2) the forecasting process itself, which is a conversion step similar to physical production, and 3) the outputs, which are forecasts containing the "four Rs": reasoned, reasonable, reviewed frequently, and reflecting the total demand. Figure 3-2 shows this graphically, and please note: The word *accurate* does not appear. We'll have more — a lot more — to say about the accuracy issue in the next chapter.

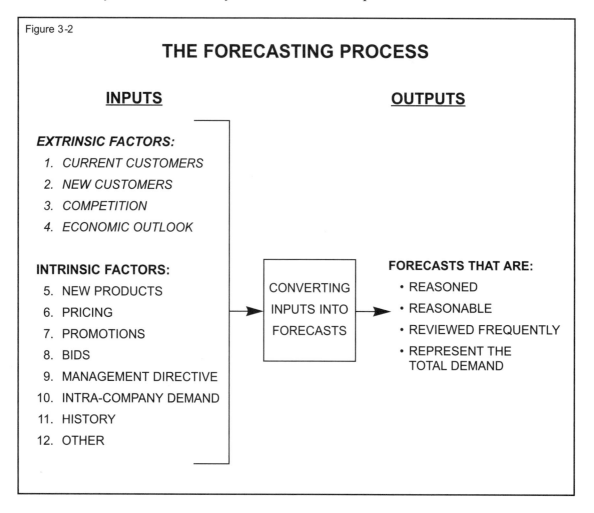

Figure 3-2

THE FORECASTING PROCESS

INPUTS — OUTPUTS

EXTRINSIC FACTORS:
1. *CURRENT CUSTOMERS*
2. *NEW CUSTOMERS*
3. *COMPETITION*
4. *ECONOMIC OUTLOOK*

INTRINSIC FACTORS:
5. NEW PRODUCTS
6. PRICING
7. PROMOTIONS
8. BIDS
9. MANAGEMENT DIRECTIVE
10. INTRA-COMPANY DEMAND
11. HISTORY
12. OTHER

CONVERTING INPUTS INTO FORECASTS

FORECASTS THAT ARE:
• REASONED
• REASONABLE
• REVIEWED FREQUENTLY
• REPRESENT THE TOTAL DEMAND

A word about the first two of the four Rs: reasoned and reasonable. Fred the forecaster is discussing the forecast with Betty, his boss.

Betty: *Fred, am I reading this right? The new forecast for large widgets is double what we did last year.*

Fred: *That's right, boss.*

Betty: *But Fred, we already have about 75 percent of that market. To double our business means the market would have to grow a lot and we'd have to increase our share to near 100 percent.*

Fred: *Oh, I don't know about that. This is what the forecasting software came up with.*

Fred flunks. His forecast for large widgets is not reasoned — he hasn't thought it through — nor reasonable — it doesn't make any sense.

Being reasoned and reasonable means that it makes sense based on past history, the current situation, and what is expected to change in the future. Fred and Betty and their colleagues should be looking at data describing the size of the large widget market, its composition, its behavior in the past, along with any industry-wide projections for the future from trade groups and/or government agencies. Before developing a specific forecast, they might observe their historical share of the total market, documenting the competitive advantages and disadvantages that made it so. They could then predict the future in aggregate based on reasoned and reasonable assumptions along with specific plans about the future.

As this aggregated volume forecast moves toward the Planning Time Fence, they would need to convert it to a detailed forecast. This would be done in one of two ways:

- Break the volume forecast down into a mix forecast, or

- Forecast the individual items separately, and then total them up to ensure that the sum of the detailed mix forecast equals the volume forecast.

In Chapter 1, Figure 1-2 shows the relationship between the volume forecast and the mix forecast. To round out the picture, we've added to that display in Figure 3-3. Here we see the big picture: the market as a whole, our share of that market, and our *assumptions* — why we expect the future to look the way we're forecasting it.

In most cases, best practice is to start with the big picture: the projected size of the entire market for this class of product. Then, based on our historical share of that market, how much can we reasonably expect to capture in the future? Once this big picture is developed, it should be updated as required by new data and new developments. Some companies employing a formal Sales & Operations Planning process will formally review the "big picture" forecast routinely as they go through the fiscal year.

Inputs

Let's first look at the inputs we saw in Figure 3-2. The first four — current customers, new customers, competition, and the economic outlook — are sometimes referred to as extrinsic factors. They exist outside of one's own company and, as such, their impact is usually more difficult to predict.

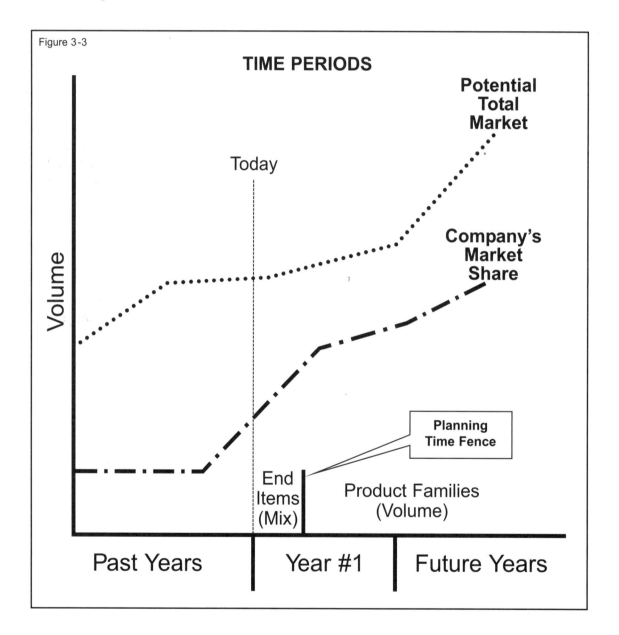

Figure 3-3

1. Current Customers

In our experience, this category is like the little girl with the curl in the middle of her forehead: When it's good it's very good; when it's bad it's horrid. Some customers, often manufacturers themselves, are so out-of-control internally that they don't have a clue as to what they're going to be needing in the future. Sometimes, their medium-to-long-range requirements are generated from dysfunctional material planning processes (bad inventory records, unstable Master Schedule, lousy bills of material) and as a result, they bear little relationship to what will actually be needed. One bit of good news here is that the number of these companies is decreasing.

The other side of the coin is a customer whose people really know what they're doing. Their planning and reordering processes are working well and they can provide good projections of what they'll actually need in the future. They're cooperative, and frequently engage in a process known as *collaborative forecasting*. This process, some-times called collaborative planning and forecasting review (CPFR), means just what it says: doing the forecasting in close collaboration with customers and *suppliers*. In some respects, it's nothing new. (One of the authors did a bit of this many years ago while in sales with General Motors.) On the other hand, this approach — used to its full potential — can represent a significantly better process to capture future demand from customers. How is it different from what we did thirty years ago? It's more structured, more formal, and it can eliminate the need for "blind forecasting" by the supplier. There is an expectation on the part of both parties — customer and supplier — that the process will help both parties to help each other. The phrase *win-win* comes to mind.

2. New Customers

These are customers that you haven't got yet, but expect to have soon. Forecasting future demand for this category can be very difficult, and that leads some companies to not forecast them at all. Understandably they're reluctant to commit resources to a customer that's still in the uncertain category. Other companies, often those with long lead times for capacity and/or materials, will forecast this type of new business and sometimes attach a probability percentage to the forecast. This can help with long range planning without necessarily making any commitments to specific products.

3. Competition

This can be both easy and hard. Knowledge of competitors' recent moves is usually not terribly difficult to learn and therefore to factor into the forecasts. On the other hand, knowledge of competitors' future plans can be very hard to come by, one exception being pre-announcements of new products, price changes, and the like. Companies with good forecasting processes typically keep a sharp eye on the competition.

4. Economic Outlook

Ask ten economists where the economy is headed, and you might get a dozen answers. On the other hand, economic outlook can play an important role in many companies' forecasts, and should not be neglected simply because of the economy's inherent uncertainty. Projections of housing starts, commercial construction, automobile sales, employment levels, changes in income levels, demographic changes — these and many other factors can play important roles in the forecast. Good forecasters will, where appropriate, make extensive use of them[1].

Now for the intrinsic factors, the ones existing primarily within the company itself.

5. New Products

It goes without saying that new products are usually very difficult to forecast. Not only that, the impact of new products and new technology on demand for existing products must also be considered, and that too can be quite a challenge. It's important to estimate the extent to which the new product will cannibalize sales of existing ones.

Because of the inherent difficulties in forecasting new products, some companies try to reduce their reliance on new product forecasts as much as possible. They may come up with a number or a range that might be off by an order of magnitude in either direction: The forecast may easily turn out to be half of the actual sales or, quite possibly, double what is actually sold.

Therefore, these companies might view that initial number merely as a point of departure and concentrate their efforts on the supply side. For example, they may have a build program that says: "Let's have X percent of the forecast produced by this point in time. We'll watch actual sales very closely and make a decision whether to continue to produce

---

[1] For some products, the relationship between the economy and future sales are inverse: Sales increase during a down economy. Lower-priced beer and wine come to mind.

per this plan, or to increase or decrease the build rate. Down the road, if and when things stabilize, we'll get into a normal forecasting mode with this new product."

6. Pricing

Price changes — their timing and the timing of their announcement — frequently influence demand and thus should be explicitly considered in the forecasting process.

7. Promotions

Promotions, accelerated advertising, and so on are done to influence customer demand. Thus their expected impact should be explicitly factored into the forecast.

8. Bids

In some companies, a large amount of customer demand comes in through the bidding process. The company's open bids, perhaps each carrying a probability percentage of capturing the order, may provide a good handle on future demand.

9. Management Directive

This can be a tough one. Here's an example of what we mean:

> Vice President of Sales & Marketing: *"Boss, here's our sales forecast for next year: $450 million.*
> President: *"I'm sorry. I can't hear you. You're very faint."*

Some time later.

> VP: *"Boss, I've got our new forecast here: $475 million.*
> President: *"I still can't hear you. Your voice is so faint that it's almost like you're . . . out the door."*

Some time later.

> VP: *"Boss, here's our new forecast: $500 million.*
> President: *"Terrific! That's great. Now just make sure you sell it."*

In many companies, this scenario — the top management decree — is a way of life. But, all is not lost when this happens. Frequently what the president is saying is that the consequences of a lower forecast are severe and painful, and that the company should put things in place to avoid that. The question then becomes: What do we have to do to make it happen? The job of people in Sales & Marketing is to recognize this and develop detailed marketing and sales plans to do it. The wrong response is to change the numbers and nothing else.

Tom Kilgore from Procter & Gamble says: "It's essential to make the gap visible and help the president see that his or her expectation is not reasonable unless more resources — product, promotion, pricing, and so forth — are provided." More about this in Chapter 6, when we talk about Sales & Operations Planning.

10. Intra-Company Demand

Demand from sister divisions, plants within the same division, export, sampling programs, and the like must be explicitly recognized in the forecast. If not, the forecast will be incomplete. Then, when the demand materializes, surprises will occur and they will not be good surprises. Frequently this kind of demand is large and lumpy; it comes infrequently and in big bunches. Not formally recognizing it ahead of time in the forecast can make a difficult situation much worse.

11. History

This refers to data from past sales, and it is an important input. The ability to make statistical projections based on past history is a key element in many companies' forecasting processes. However, we believe that it's been overemphasized, with the result that other, equally or more important determinants of future customer demand have been given insufficient attention or overlooked completely. Our bottom line: History is important, but it is only one of the dozen or so inputs to the forecasting process. Furthermore, for most companies, it is not the most important input. We believe that, for many companies, statistical forecasting can be a big help when blended intelligently with the other elements that bear on future customer demand. (See Appendix H for a discussion of the widely used statistical forecasting technique known as Exponential Smoothing.)

A question that sometimes arises is whether it's better to use historical data that reflects incoming demand (bookings), or alternatively, data that reflects actual sales (shipments, billings). Bookings data or shipment data, that is the question. Well, in almost all cases, demand data is preferable. One main reason is that demand data reflects more clearly what the customers wanted; it is not distorted by backorders, late shipments, partial shipments, cancellations, and the like. This is important, because distorted data can certainly degrade the forecasts that are made from it.

Some companies just getting started with statistical forecasting face a dilemma: They can't use demand data because they haven't saved it. Does this mean they have to use shipment data forever? Not at all. They can get started using shipments as the basis for their statistical forecasts, being careful to review and adjust statistical forecasts made on those products with a history of shortages and other demand/supply problems. Going forward, they save the demand data and phase that in as the basis for future forecasts.

One last word on history: Don't overlook it. We can remember the president of a consumer products company complaining about the unpredictability of demand and the poor job they did in forecasting a recent sales promotion. We asked him if he had looked at the historical pattern of prior promotions that were similar. His face went blank, and then he smiled as the light bulb went on. He agreed that looking at data from the earlier promotions probably would have:

1. helped them make a better forecast and thus

2. caused them to have more product available for the promotion and thus

3. enabled them to sell more product and thus

4. caused them to make more money.

Good forecasting — reasoned, reasonable, etc. — can positively impact both your top and bottom lines. And you can take that to the bank.

12. Other

You may have some "others" in your forecasting situation, some important inputs that we haven't mentioned. Here's an example: A friend of ours worked in the market research department of a piano manufacturer. He discovered a very helpful predictor of total piano sales: the birth rate with an eight-to-ten year lag. When you think about it, it figures. When little Susie gets to be about eight years old or so, Mom and Dad start thinking about buying her a piano. Do you have any of these "other" kinds of elements that may help you develop better forecasts?

Weather, as forecasted in the Farmers' Almanac, can play a role in the forecasting of some products. Companies in agriculture, lawn products, snow removal equipment and supplies, and so forth frequently benefit from adding in an allowance for what the weather is expected to be.

Companies in the high-tech world face a substantial challenge. Their rate of new product introduction is high, product life cycles are short, and end-of-life forecasting is an important activity. Furthermore, on occasion their entire product line can be impacted (threatened?) by new technological developments, some of which may be coming from their own R&D resources or extrinsically, from outside the company.

The Forecasting Process

Let's go back to our production analogy. The process of converting raw materials into finished products requires not only materials but three additional "m's": manpower, machinery, and methods. (See Figure 3-4.)

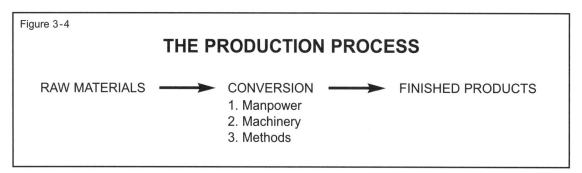

Figure 3-4

THE PRODUCTION PROCESS

RAW MATERIALS ⟶ CONVERSION ⟶ FINISHED PRODUCTS
1. Manpower
2. Machinery
3. Methods

Well, pretty much the same thing applies to the process of making forecasts. In addition to the inputs we've just seen, this conversion activity requires people, computer software and hardware (almost always), and structured steps for performing the task. See Figure 3-5.

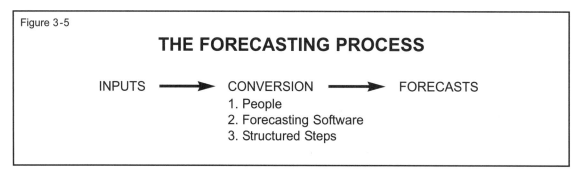

Figure 3-5

THE FORECASTING PROCESS

INPUTS ⟶ CONVERSION ⟶ FORECASTS
1. People
2. Forecasting Software
3. Structured Steps

Let's look at each of these three elements in the forecasting process.

1. People

This book is largely about people. We've talked extensively about the people aspect of forecasting in prior chapters and we'll do more of the same in the chapters to come. Here we'd like to look at some of the decisions that face the people who will be involved in the forecasting process.

Forecast Frequency

For a formal review and update, the most commonly used frequency is once per month. For most companies in most situations, a monthly cycle works well. Of course, if the demand picture undergoes major changes mid-month, the forecast should be updated at that time. For most companies, forecasting less frequently than once per month can lead to problems. Most businesses are simply too fast-paced and dynamic to allow for, say, a ninety-day gap between formal reviews of the forecast.

Forecasting more frequently than once per month can work well, but before you jump into that, be sure you're doing it for the right reasons. We've seen companies changing the forecast very frequently in order to effect changes directly into the near-term production line-up. This is almost always a result of not having a good scheduling system, so they manipulate the forecast (a statement of demand) to directly affect production, which of course is supply. It is not a good practice, and it almost never yields good results.

Company S produces consumer packaged goods with a highly seasonal sales curve. They used to change the forecast frequently, in the very near term. What do you think the impact was on the plants and suppliers? It drove them crazy. There were constant changes: Stop that, start this, increase that, decrease this. As we learned more about what they were doing, we saw why: Their master scheduling and plant scheduling processes were right out of the 1950s. The Sales & Marketing folks felt their only chance of getting the right stuff produced was to constantly change the forecast. It was the informational equivalent of using a saw to drive nails.

The good news is they don't do that anymore. They have a good resource planning system in place and can really manage their Master Schedule and plant schedules. Today they change the forecast far less frequently, run the plant more efficiently, and provide far better customer service than before.

On the other hand, some companies who excel at Continuous Replenishment (CR) update their "forecasts" a number of times per week. Typically they're receiving point-of-sale data from their larger customers, and thus can see through the customers' distribution systems right into the retail stores. They can recalculate their customers' expected demands over the next few days, reset their finishing schedules, and produce. These companies usually don't change their monthly forecast at each update, but rather they consume it. We'll talk more about forecast consumption in Chapter 7.

This is probably beyond the scope of many companies' capabilities today. Some possible exceptions might be high volume consumer goods companies or medical suppliers; these folks have developed a highly integrated supply chain and replenishment processes. Unless you're really good at it, go with a frequency of once per month for your forecast updates. You can always go to a higher forecast frequency later if you determine that will help. For the balance of this chapter and beyond, we'll assume a monthly forecasting cycle.

Forecast Interval

This refers to how "wide" a time period is used: weekly, monthly, quarterly, or whatever. When forecasting for the next year, for example, is the result 52 individual forecasts, each representing one week? Or 12, each covering a month? Or four, one per quarter?

Most companies that are good at forecasting use a monthly forecast interval, and that seems to work quite well. Forecasting in weekly increments can result in lots of numbers when projected for a year or more into the future and, what's worse, may impart a sense of false precision. It doesn't make sense to us to generate this degree of detail when the accuracy is no better — and may quite possibly be worse — than generating a monthly and dividing by 4, 4.3, or 5.

Quarterly numbers make it very difficult to determine seasonal fluctuations. The monthly approach wins by default.

Right now some of you might be thinking: Okay, but don't we need weekly forecasts for the Master Schedule?[2] Well, you surely do. And the way that most companies get weekly forecast numbers is simply to chop up the monthly forecasts into weekly increments using some agreed upon pattern for translating the months into weeks.

Forecast Horizon

How far into the future should the forecast go? A week, a month, a quarter? Well, the correct answer for most companies will be "none of the above." If the company is truly going to operate with only one forecast, then it must cover more than the next year (at certain times, anyway).

The good news is that you're almost certainly doing this already. At least once per year, you're probably forecasting 15 or more months into the future. That's when you do the budget for next year. Typically you start working on the budget three or more months prior

---

[2] We'll discuss the role of the Master Schedule in Chapter 6. For now, let's just say that it's the primary schedule driving customer order promising, production, and procurement.

to the end of the current fiscal year. Let's say that World Wide Widget's fiscal year begins January 1. Sometime in late summer or early fall they'll go to work on the upcoming budget, and one of the first things they'll do is to develop a forecast for the upcoming fiscal year: January through December. They now have about 15 months of forward forecast.

We're proposing that World Wide and other companies do it this way every month. Figure on a 12-to-18 month or greater forecast horizon, and forecast out that far every month. For each month that goes by, add another month. Or, as some companies do, add three months of forecast once each quarter.

A caveat: 12 to 15 months may not be enough. Companies with long lead times for facilities, equipment, materials, and/or highly trained people will need more of a horizon. For example, companies in businesses like aerospace or chemicals go out three years, and there are probably others with a need for even longer projections.

Sometimes people question the need to have that long a horizon available all year. They point out that certainly you need that much at budget time, but not for the entire year. Here's our response:

1. For effective financial planning, you'll need a minimum of 12 months. The reason: to span the current fiscal year. During the first month of the year (January in the case of World Wide), the sales projection for the entire fiscal year is all forecast. In February, it's one month of actual sales (January) and 11 months of forecast. In August, it's seven months of actual sales plus five forecast.

   Does it make sense to have a different forecast horizon for each month of the fiscal year? We think not. We recommend that companies develop a routine process, to be done the same way each month.

   Further, in August, before World Wide starts on next year's budget, they have only five months of future forecast. Is this enough upon which to base effective decisions? Often it's not. The frequent result: scrambling for numbers, less effective decision-making, or perhaps making no decision at all.

2. Another benefit of a longer forecast horizon is the learning curve effect. Doing this process monthly will help the forecasters do a better job forecasting out into the future than they'd be able to do if they did it only once per year. Will these forecasts be highly accurate? We doubt it very much. But, they don't have to be highly accurate; their role is to give overall direction, not specific details.

3. Capacity issues could also be a factor here. Shifts in volume during the year could generate the need for equipment, or possibly people, with long acquisition lead times. It's far better not to wait until the annual planning cycle to discover those kinds of things.

We prefer 15 months versus 12 months because at least once per year, at budget time, you'll need to go out 15 months. In our experience, it's only a little more work to routinely deal with a 15-month horizon as opposed to 12, but a 15-month forecast horizon makes the budgeting process a lot easier and more routine.

2. Forecasting Software

The second component of the forecasting process is software. Your authors believe in the ABC principle as it relates to business systems and decision-making processes. This is a variation of Pareto's Law, which concerns the vital few and the less important many. This is often seen in inventory management: The relatively few A items are the ones with high impact, dollars or otherwise, while the many C items have low impact. The B items are the ones in the middle. An important point about the C items: They're essential, frequently needed to make a shipment. So the issue is not one of necessity, but one of impact and importance. The C items are essential, but of less significance.

The ABC approach also applies to forecasting processes:

The C item is the computer software and hardware.
Essential, but not the critically important item.

The B item is the data.
The validity and utility of the input data is of
more significance than the computer.

The A item is the people.
The success of a forecasting improvement initiative
will depend almost totally on the people:
their dedication, their willingness, their knowledge.

More on the A item later. For now let's focus on the C item, specifically the software, and start with a caveat: When we refer to forecasting software, we are not talking about highly sophisticated econometric models and other approaches sometimes used by very large corporations, government agencies, and so forth. Those tools are beyond the scope of this book. Forecasting software, as we use it here, refers to a set of programs to do several things: to make statistical projections and to handle data.

Statistical Projections

The approach here is to utilize statistical methods to project the future from the past. These methods span the gamut from very simple moving averages all the way to very sophisticated, complex algorithms such as adaptive exponential smoothing or regression analysis.

What is the best approach? We come down perhaps somewhere in the middle of that range, leaning towards the side of simplicity and ease of understanding. Why? Because of the A item: the people. If all of the forecasters in your company have masters degrees in advanced statistics, go for it! Get as much forecasting horsepower as you can, and don't worry about complexity and difficulty of understanding.

On the other hand, if most of your people aren't that sophisticated, then you'll be well advised to focus on simplicity and ease of understanding — perhaps at the cost of giving up some power. Pete Skurla of the Oliver Wight organization says it well: "If you can't explain what the forecasting software is doing, don't use it." Some of the more popular and more effective forecasting software is quite simple and easy to understand, as well as easy to explain to non-statisticians.

One of the pioneers in the forecasting field is Bernie Smith. He developed a forecasting process called Focus Forecasting[3] that combines simplicity with a capability to utilize a number of different forecast models simultaneously. After the month is over and actual sales for the month are known, the software computes the forecast error generated by each of the various models over the last quarter, and then informs the user which one would have had the lowest accumulated error. The user can then decide to change to a new model or continue with the current one. Today there are several forecasting packages available utilizing a similar approach. And of course, there are other packages utilizing other approaches. Those of you with interest in this area may want to look at Appendix B: Classification of Forecasting Methodologies, and Appendix C: Listing of Forecasting Software Suppliers.

---

[3] Bernard T. Smith, *Focus Forecasting.* Boston, MA: CBI Publishing, 1978.

Data Handling

This refers to the ability of the software to store, maintain, display, aggregate, and disaggregate data. Don't overlook this seemingly mundane function if and when you're searching for forecasting software. The ability to accumulate data into larger entities, to "slice and dice" it into smaller ones, to view the same basic forecasts in a number of different ways — for Operations, for Finance, and for Sales & Marketing — these are very important capabilities for almost all companies.

In fact, some companies claim that the benefits they receive from these data handling capabilities exceed those of the statistical forecasting piece of the software package. This can be particularly true for companies whose products are largely make-to-order versus make-to-stock, where statistical projections may be of less importance; the ability to view forecast data by customer and then combine it into larger entities can be extremely helpful.

We'll talk more about this important aspect of forecasting software in Chapter 5, where we'll discuss the proper level of detail. For the time being, as we go through the next section, try not to worry about the amount of detail and hence, work involved. There are ways to make the forecasting process workable in virtually any company, without having to devote large amounts of resources (people, time, money) to it.

3. Structured Steps

The third element, structured steps in the forecasting process, is important, because these steps are the vehicle for the people — the A item — to do their jobs.

Data Gathering and Preparation

There are two parts to this step, one being the activities done prior to the end of the month and the other being those things done following the month's end.

1. Prior to month-end. It's important to do as much as possible prior to the end of the month, so that the subsequent steps in the process — forecast development, decision-making and authorization — are not delayed. There is urgency to getting the entire forecasting process wrapped up quickly, so that the new forecast can serve as timely input to planning activities that need to take place in Operations, in Finance, and perhaps elsewhere. Happily, almost all of the inputs to the forecasting process can be addressed prior to the month's end.

2. <u>After month-end</u>. One notable exception to the last statement is history, which normally can't be wrapped up until the month is over and the complete month's worth of data is known[4]. It's particularly important to have the full month's data as input to what happens next: running statistical forecasting system to get new projections, and also generating the input media (electronic or otherwise) for marketing folks, field salespeople and others to use in communicating their forecasts.

A caveat: Don't assume that your demand data is accurate. In some companies this can be a problem, particularly when dealing with bookings data (incoming orders) as opposed to sales data (shipments). Shipment data is usually very solid, as invoices are generated from them, but bookings may not be quite as stable. Most companies don't have a major problem here, but whatever demand data is used should be checked to verify that the numbers are valid.

Data gathering and preparation should be completed within a day or two following the end of the month, the reason being the urgency cited above. In our experience, companies who are serious about doing a first-rate job of forecasting find this timing very achievable.

Forecast Generation

The forecast generation step can involve:

- running the statistical forecasting software, or

- collating feedback from the field sales forecast, or

- both of the above.

This is the foundation step, which makes possible all that follows. Appendix G shows a sample of a statistical forecast projection and a sample worksheet used for feedback from the field sales force.

---

[4] One exception to this is the company whose products are make-to-order and has a complete backlog for at least the next month. This type of company knows the total demand (via its bookings) for the upcoming month before the prior month is over. Thus it can get a jump on its forecasting work before month end.

Another exception is a company with a weekly forecasting cycle and interval, which can readily separate its forecast cycle from the start of the month.

Volume and Mix Reconciliation #1

As we said earlier, the volume forecast (families) and the mix forecast (end items) must be one and the same. They're merely different expressions of the same forecast. Thus they need to be reconciled, so that they agree. Some companies derive the mix forecast directly from the aggregate volume forecast, and that's fine. Another approach is to forecast in aggregate and also to forecast separately at the detailed, mix level. In these cases, there needs to be a formal reconciliation step here to ensure that the two sets of numbers are in fact one — that they're saying the same thing.

Applying Judgment

In most companies, this step constitutes the "heavy lifting" of the forecast cycle. It may be done by people with the job title of demand manager, demand/supply planner, fore-cast analyst — or it may be done within the product management group by the product manager(s) or one of his or her assistants.

There's a lot more to this step than merely accepting the output from the statistical forecasting software. It should involve an analysis and subsequent synthesis of all the relevant inputs shown earlier in Figure 3-2: customers, competition, the economy, new product plans, pricing changes and promotions, intra-company demand, and so forth. The resulting set of forecast numbers is a blend of what's come out of the statistical forecasting process, feedback from the field, and other relevant extrinsic and intrinsic factors.

Volume and Mix Reconciliation #2

After "applying judgment," some of the forecasts will be different. It's once again necessary to get the volume forecast and the mix forecast reconciled, so that they're equal and we're still operating with one set of forecast numbers.

Documenting Assumptions

This initial forecast needs to contain more than just the numerical data relating to future demand. To be truly effective, it needs to show the *assumptions* that underlie the forecasts. Documenting assumptions is a critically important part of the overall forecasting process, for two reasons:

1. <u>Bulletproofing and Buy-In</u>: A number of people, up to and including at least the VP of Sales & Marketing, will be reviewing the new forecast prior to its authorization. Having the assumptions visible to everyone involved in that process enables these folks to question these assumptions, modify them, override them, or — at a minimum — accept them. These assumptions, and thus the forecasts based on them, acquire a wide buy-in as they go through this process. No longer is it just the product manager whose butt is on the line for this forecast. A number of key players are now involved.

2. <u>Explanation and Learning</u>: Frequently people scratch their heads and say: "How did we miss the forecast by that much? What were we thinking?" This occurs after the period is over and actual sales are known. Well, being able to see the assumptions upon which the forecast was made can help to answer those kinds of questions. On forecasts that were off by a lot, documented assumptions can help show how the forecast went wrong. We can learn from it and perhaps avoid the same mistake in the future.

Documenting assumptions is an essential part of a first-rate forecasting process.

Decision-Making and Authorization

Forecasting is really all about decision-making.

- First, the person operating the statistical forecasting system decides which statistical models to employ, what forecast parameters to use, and perhaps how much weight to give to the various extrinsic and intrinsic factors. Also, the field salespeople, preferably in conjunction with their customers, decide what is the most likely future sales volume for their accounts.

- Next, product management people review all of the above and decide what the forecasts should be, i.e., what will be the level of future sales. This, in effect, constitutes their recommendations to senior management.

- Lastly, the senior executive in charge of sales and marketing reviews the new forecast and decides whether to authorize it as is, or to make modifications prior to its release to other parts of the company. This is an essential step; this authorization validates the forecast numbers, enabling them to become truly Sales & Marketing's best effort at projecting the future volume of business. These steps are recapped in Figure 3-6.

Some people call the output from this last step the "consensus forecast." This term, which we happen to like, implies that the forecast now is agreed-upon following development and review by the key players. Please note: Consensus does not mean unanimity. There may be people who would prefer a different number but once consensus is reached, all the players need to get behind the plan and support it.

Volume and Mix Reconciliation #3

Any changes made in the decision-making and authorization step need to be reflected in the appropriate mix or volume forecasts.

Figure 3-6

STRUCTURED STEPS IN THE FORECASTING PROCESS

Data Gathering and Preparation

Forecast Generation

Volume and Mix Reconciliation #1

Applying Judgment

Volume and Mix Reconciliation #2

Documenting Assumptions

Decision-Making and Authorization

Volume and Mix Reconciliation #3

Gripes and Tips

Gripe: *It's impossible to make any sense out of this forecasting stuff.* In response we offer two principles:

Principle #4: The forecast can and must make sense based on the big picture: economic outlook, industry trends, market share, and so on.

Principle #5: Better processes yield better results; better forecasting processes yield better forecasts.

In this chapter, we've discussed the inputs to forecasting and the conversion (forecasting) step itself. Coming up next, we'll cover the outputs from that process, including the answer to that dreaded question: How accurate should the forecast be?

CHAPTER 4

ACCURACY

Gripe: *If we could just get an accurate forecast,*
it would solve all our problems.

Let's start this chapter with a question-and-answer session between your two authors.

BOB: *Have you ever been asked the question: How accurate should the forecast be?*

TOM: *Only about ten thousand times. At least it seems that way.*

BOB: *And what do you say in response?*

TOM: *The first thing I do is wince. Then I explain that I try never to use the word forecast and the word accurate in the same sentence.*

BOB: *That's a radical statement!*

TOM: *Yeah, and it's not totally tongue-in-cheek. What I'm getting at is that forecast accuracy may be a desirable goal, but harping about forecast accuracy is not the way to get there.*

BOB: *Why not?*

TOM: *Because it's a turnoff for the people who have to do the forecasting. During my time in industry, I had a couple of tours in Marketing. I got fed up with being hammered about how inaccurate my forecasts were. It was a thankless job: I always got nailed for my bad forecasts but never — not once — did I get an "attaboy" or a pat on the back for a good forecast. How happy was I to sit down once a month and put together a bunch of numbers that I knew I'd get beat up for? Not very.*

Let me hasten to add that I believe that accurate forecasts are wonderful things and they bring big benefits: better customer service, less inventory, less investment in excess "flex" capacity, fewer changeovers, and more. There's no issue about the desirability of accurate forecasts; it's how you get there.

Another irony is that everyone knows that the forecast is going to be wrong. We all know that, but still many people complain about the lack of accuracy in the forecasts.

In an earlier book[1], one of your authors said this: "People who routinely criticize the forecasters for their inaccuracy might ask themselves a few basic questions. First, if the Sales & Marketing people could predict the future with great accuracy, do you really think they'd be working for a living? Would they be knocking themselves out for forty or fifty or more hours per week? Of course not. If they could predict the future with great accuracy, where would they be? At the racetrack. And if the track were closed? They'd be home on their PCs, trading in stock options and speculating on pork-belly futures."

So that's one good reason why we're uncomfortable with trying to answer the question: How accurate should the forecast be? Another reason is that it's impossible. There is no one answer to that question. It depends.

Underlying Variability

It's impossible to answer the forecast accuracy question because the maximum level of forecast accuracy is often a function of the variability of the data itself. Let's hear why from Professor George Johnson of the Rochester Institute of Technology, who used the example of driving a tired, old car that "has given me an average of 17 miles per gallon on the road and never gone above 20 nor below 14 mpg under normal operating conditions. Thus the normal range of highway mpg is 14–20 with an average of 17. I forecast 17 mpg for my next trip with this car. At trip end, I compute the mpg actually is 14. I'm not surprised because it has done this before under typical operating conditions."[2]

He pointed out that he's OK with 14 actual mpg against his forecast of 17, but perhaps others ("management") might not be. After all, if the rules of the game specify +/- 15 percent, then he's outside of the lower limit of 14.45 (17 mpg times 15% = 2.55 mpg). Here's George again: "I'm going to get criticized. But wait a minute. I operated the car correctly — did what I was supposed to do — and the outcome was the result of 'common' causes of variation. It's not fair that I get criticized. The car and I were doing the best we could do under the circumstances. After being unreasonably criticized a few times, I start to get motivated to coast down hills, sneak a little extra gas into the tank, and play the system in other ways so I don't get penalized for things I can't control. This is not the best way to use my time (or company resources), but it will keep me out of trouble."

[1] Wallace, Thomas F. *Sales & Operations Planning—The How-To Handbook.* Cincinnati, OH: T.F. Wallace & Company, 1999.

[2] Johnson, George. Dear APICS. *APICS: The Performance Advantage*, April 1999, (p. 22)

A lot of companies have salespeople who feel the same way — not about their forecasts of car mileage of course, but rather their sales forecasts. Arbitrary standards for forecast accuracy that don't take into account the underlying variability are almost always a bad idea.

George Johnson then made a point that we've already heard but it is certainly worth repeating: *forecasting is a process*, so the issue here is one of *process control and improvement*. Our response to that: right on! This is the necessary view, but one that many people fail to adopt when talking about forecasting. If we take a process view towards forecasting, then we can start to talk about inputs, outputs, and process error.

He also pointed out that *processes have inherent variation, and because forecasting is a process there will be some variability.* This means that some degree of forecast error is inevitable. Some companies disregard this factor and push their Marketing and Sales people to make super-accurate forecasts. We've seen this approach result in counter-productive behavior. Examples range from switching off (refusing to forecast because it's a no-win deal and they're tired of getting beat up) to forecasting too frequently (updating the forecast every few days based on the last few days' orders). Quality guru W. Edwards Deming referred to this as "tampering" — being given incentives to do the wrong thing and thus doing it. Either of these kinds of behavior can drive Manufacturing and Purchasing crazy.

Total Quality Management Tools

Within the body of knowledge known as Total Quality Management (TQM), there are powerful tools with which to improve processes — tools like Pareto charts, cause-and-effect (Fishbone) diagrams, run charts, control charts, and many more.

Here's the important point: These kinds of tools can be used to improve forecasting processes as well as physical processes for producing products. And they are being used today. In fact, we're starting to see these tools included in forecasting software packages, and that's certainly a positive development. If you're shopping for forecasting software, we recommend that you add TQM problem solving tools to your wish list. The existence of these tools in a given package might not be a sufficient reason to buy that package, but their availability may tilt the decision in favor of that package in a close competition.

On the other hand, if you already have forecasting software and it doesn't contain these tools, be of good cheer. You probably have all of the necessary statistical quality software you might need within the company (and more importantly, people who are knowledgeable in the use of these tools). They're most likely to be found in the Quality Assurance department and possibly elsewhere throughout the organization. You may want to enlist their help as you go about improving your forecasting processes.

This is a managerial book, not a technical one, so delving into the mechanics of process improvement tools is outside its scope. If you want to learn more, an excellent source is a booklet called "The Memory Jogger — A Pocket Guide for Continuous Improvement" available from Goal/QPC in Methuen, MA.

Reduce Forecast Error

Let's get another forecasting principle on the table: **The best way to increase forecast accuracy is to focus on reducing forecast error.** Some of you are probably thinking, "Isn't this just semantics? Isn't reducing forecast error the same thing as increasing accuracy?" Well yes, strictly speaking, you're right. But the reason we stress this point is that focusing on forecast error reduction does several things:

1. It's a less emotionally charged term than forecast accuracy. In our experience, Sales & Marketing people react more positively to the task of reducing forecast error.

2. When we think in terms of forecast error, variability of demand data, and variability of processes, then we can start to apply proven techniques from the fields of statistics and quality control.

3. Focusing on forecast error makes it easier to attack the worst kind of forecast error: bias.

We'll have more to say on bias in just a bit. First, however, it's time for a quiz.

Which Is Best?

Forecast and actual demand data for three products are shown in Figure 4-1. The question we'd like you to answer is which of these three forecasts has the lowest error or, if you like, which one is the most accurate? (Please note: This is not a trick question.) Well, it's pretty obvious that Product Z is the most accurate. Its errors are substantially lower than the other two. That one was easy, but now let's make it a little tougher: Which of the other two products, X or Y, is the most accurate?

Now the answer isn't so clear. Some people might pick Product X, because its average error is five. Product Y has an average error of around 14, almost three times that of X.

Figure 4-1

WHICH FORECAST IS THE MOST ACCURATE?

PRODUCT X	1	2	3	4	5
FORECAST	100	105	110	115	120
ACTUAL	105	108	119	118	125

PRODUCT Y	1	2	3	4	5
FORECAST	100	100	100	100	100
ACTUAL	90	120	85	115	90

PRODUCT Z	1	2	3	4	5
FORECAST	100	100	100	100	100
ACTUAL	101	99	100	99	101

On the other hand, some of you might disagree, using the following logic: Product Y is the more accurate of the two because its accumulated error over time is zero; Product X's accumulated error for these five periods is +25 (see Figure 4-2).

Figure 4-2

WHICH FORECAST IS THE MOST ACCURATE?

PRODUCT X	1	2	3	4	5	
FORECAST	100	105	110	115	120	
ACTUAL	105	108	119	118	125	
VARIABILITY (MAD)	|5|	|3|	|9|	|3|	|5|	AVG = |5|
BIAS (RFSE)	+5	+8	+17	+20	+25	

PRODUCT Y	1	2	3	4	5	
FORECAST	100	100	100	100	100	
ACTUAL	90	120	85	115	90	
VARIABILITY (MAD)	|10|	|10|	|15|	|15|	|10|	AVG = |12|
BIAS (RFSE)	-10	+10	-5	+10	0	

Let's explain two of the terms used in Figure 4-2.

1. Variability is the average forecast error per period, sometimes called Mean Absolute Deviation[3] (MAD). It measures randomness, i.e., the variation of actual sales from forecast, *irrespective* of whether that variation is plus or minus. For example, Product Y's absolute error (ignoring plus or minus) is 60, divided by the number of periods, five, equals 12.

2. Bias is the running, accumulated forecast error plus or minus. It's also called Running Sum of Forecast Error (RFSE) or Sum of Deviations (SOD).

Now, back to some more questions. This time, you ask the questions and your friendly authors will attempt to answer.

Reader: *Which of these two forecasts is "more accurate?"*

Friendly authors: *We don't know.*

Reader: *Which of these two forecasts has the lower forecast error?*

FAs: *It depends (on which error measure is used).*

Reader: *Is there anything you guys are sure of?*

FAs: *You bet. We'd much rather supply Product Y than Product X.*

Product X has low variability but a high bias, a large accumulated error build up on the plus side. It will probably be difficult to consistently meet customer demand for Product X because the supply chain will be geared up to meet lower demand than what actually occurs. (And your friendly authors would be sorely tempted to crank in a little "Kentucky windage" into this forecast — to increase it some — on our own. Of course, as soon as we do that, we're into multiple forecasts and that's not the road to success.)

On the other hand, Product Y has high variability but zero bias. There are many products with demand patterns like this: random variation around a stable average. In cases like this, the best forecast is often one that cuts right through the middle of the demand. This is much more effective than trying to "chase" the ups and downs of a random series of numbers.

---

[3] The statistical measure of standard deviation also can be used here. MAD is easier to calculate.

To provide a buffer for those random ups and downs of demand, the MAD — or alternatively the standard deviation — can be used to calculate *safety stock*. More on this to come in Chapter 6. For now let's just say that, given some safety stock or, better yet, flexibility and short lead times, meeting customer demand for Product Y will be much less challenging than what's been happening with Product X.

One last question: What should be done with Product X to make it less challenging? After all, it's at least equally important to give good customer service with a growing product (perhaps early in the life cycle) as with a stable, mature item like Product Y. There are statistical forecasting techniques designed to deal with items trending up or down, and also with seasonal items, and virtually all forecasting software packages contain them.

And one last point: For the last two pages, we've been looking at tabular, numeric data. But you don't have to do it that way. These numbers could easily be put into graphical form, as pictures aid in comprehension. Also, the TQM tools we mentioned earlier could be profitably used for analysis here.

Stamp Out Bias

More Q & A with the authors:

TOM: *Bob, you have a rather extreme definition of forecast bias. What do you call it?*

BOB: *Bias is a forecast that's wrong on purpose.*

TOM: *Are you saying that people with biased forecasts are evil and malicious?*

BOB: *No, not at all — I'm just trying to make a point that bias is almost always caused by factors outside the forecasting process. It frequently revolves around how people are evaluated and compensated. If I consistently get "attaboys" and maybe also bonus dollars for my sales exceeding forecast, then you can be pretty sure I'm going to give you low forecasts.*

By now you've probably got the picture that we're bears on bias. Bias in the forecasts — consistently over or under — typically causes lots of problems on the supply side. If the forecast is continually low, the result is late shipments, unhappy customers, scrambling, unplanned overtime, and on and on. Conversely, a routinely high forecast can result in surplus inventories, excess capacity, layoffs, and more. Thus, principle #7: **Bias is the worst kind of forecast error; strive for zero bias.**

There's a saying: "Things that get measured get better" and we agree completely. Therefore, if the company is serious about reducing and eliminating bias, then bias should be very visible on the radar screen. To say it another way, a primary focus of the forecast measurement system should be to track and report on bias. Further, we recommend that the people responsible for the forecasts, for example product line managers, be rewarded for good performance here.

Let's take a look at World Wide Widgets. They have three product line managers: Larry LaRue, Rita Ramundo (sometimes called "Curly" because of her hair), and Paula "Mo" Morgan. Both Larry and Curly's product lines are mostly mature and have somewhat stable demand. Mo is in charge of the new consumer product line, and her products are much more difficult to forecast.

Question: Should Mo's forecast accuracy be directly compared to Larry and Curly's? Answer: no. It's virtually impossible for Mo's forecasts to be as accurate. Remember Professor George Johnson's example earlier in this chapter about driving the car? Well, Mo's forecasting challenge is the equivalent of her driving on old clunker of a car with a bad carburetor and other engine problems, while Larry and Curly are driving new machines with computer controlled fuel injection and all the rest. There's no way that Mo can do as well. Larry and Curly's average forecast error might easily be within +/- 10 percent; Mo could be lucky to do +/- 30 percent.

However, there is one area where Mo's performance can be more directly measured and related: bias. In Figure 4-3, we can see that Larry has substantially less variability than either Curly or Mo. However, we believe that Larry is doing the worst forecasting job of the three because he is consistently underforecasting; his bias is significantly higher than the others. Demand for Curly's products is less stable; it has more random ups and downs, but she's doing a better job of having her forecast "cut through the middle" of these variations. Mo also gets a thumbs up: She's dealing with a highly variable item in a pronounced uptrend but is managing to keep the bias relatively low, certainly lower than Larry.

To sum up: Measure bias, track it, report on it and, where appropriate, motivate people to minimize it. Identify the root causes of bias, which may fall into one of the following categories:

- Forecasting low in order to beat the plan and thus look good.

- Forecasting high to match the original annual plan, despite sharply changed circumstances.

- Forecasting high because Manufacturing tends to underproduce.

- Forecasting low to reduce the inventories.

- Forecasting high to guarantee good customer service.

There can be other factors causing bias. Root out the root causes. Then eliminate them. Get rid of bias. Stamp it out.

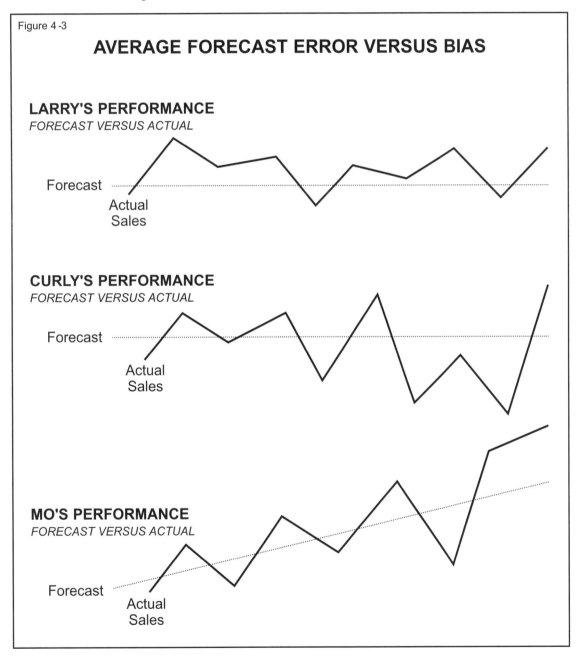

Figure 4-3

AVERAGE FORECAST ERROR VERSUS BIAS

Tracking Signal

Sometimes an item with high variability may go for two or three months in a row with its forecast error in the same direction. Thus bias seems to be building up when in reality, it's just a random event. The bias will decrease when the monthly forecast error goes in the opposite direction.

How can one avoid being "bothered" with error messages about bias when, in fact, that bias is random and temporary? That's where the tracking signal can help. It relates variability (mean absolute deviation — MAD) and bias (running sum of forecast error — RFSE).

In Figure 4-4, below, we see similar data to that shown in Figure 4-2 with one addition: the tracking signal and limits. The tracking signal is calculated by dividing the item's accumulated error build-up (bias, RFSE) by its inherent randomness (variability, MAD).

Figure 4-4

WHICH FORECAST IS THE MOST ACCURATE?

PRODUCT M

	1	2	3	4	5
FORECAST	100	100	100	100	100
ACTUAL	92	122	90	112	98
VARIABILITY (MAD)					|11|
BIAS (RFSE)	-8	+14	+4	+16	+14
TRACKING SIGNAL (RFSE/MAD)					1.3
TRACKING SIGNAL LIMIT: 3.0					

PRODUCT X

	1	2	3	4	5
FORECAST	100	105	110	115	120
ACTUAL	105	108	119	118	125
VARIABILITY (MAD)					|5|
BIAS (RFSE)	+5	+8	+17	+20	+25
TRACKING SIGNAL (RFSE/MAD)					5.0
TRACKING SIGNAL LIMIT: 3.0					

The tracking signal for Product M tells us that its bias is 1.3 times its variability (14/11) which, for a product like this, is usually a normal situation at any given point in time. We can see that the tracking signal limit has been set at 3.0, which means that as long as the bias is no more than three times the variability, the item's forecast is under control[4]. To say it another way, Product M's bias is within the pre-set limits. Product X is a whole different story. It's bias is five times the variability. It's out of control, and human intervention is clearly indicated.

Speed and Agility

Let's digress from forecasting for just a moment. In managing the supply chain, one of the challenging areas is the very mundane topic of inventory record accuracy. Effective decision support and execution systems in this field demand highly accurate inventory records; they can't function properly without them. (The phrase "garbage in garbage out" applies.) One of the best ways to have highly accurate inventory records is not to have inventory. We're not trying to be facetious. Little or no inventory in the real world makes the inventory accuracy task much less difficult.

There's a parallel in the world of forecasting: The best way to eliminate forecast error is to eliminate the need to forecast. Eliminating the need to forecast usually involves increased speed and agility. Here's an example.

Company D, a manufacturer of valves, had major forecasting problems with their largest product line. Due to a proliferation of models, the relatively flat level of sales was spread over an increasing number of stockkeeping units. As a result, forecast error was quite high, as were inventories and backorders.

In this marketplace, the standard order fulfillment time is three days. With a production lead time of two weeks, Company D had no choice but to forecast individual items, produce them, and put them into stock in anticipation of customer orders. However, by changing some production and purchasing processes, Company D became able to produce valves in *two days*[5] versus the two weeks it had taken previously. They no longer had to forecast at the mix level.

---

[4] Some users will vary the tracking signal limit by item class. They'll use a lower limit for A items and a higher one for C items. This stands to reason, because C items typically have more inherent variability. Plus they are often considered less important.

[5] This refers to the finishing (or final assembly) lead time, given availability of components.

So let's ask ourselves a few questions:

1. What happened to forecast error on these individual valves? It went to zero.

2. Why? Because the need to forecast these items went away.

3. What happened to finished good inventory? It became less than one tenth of what it had been.

4. What happened to backorders? They dropped to near zero.

Sounds like win-win-win to us.

Did the need to forecast go away completely? No, Company D still had to forecast overall volumes in order to have the work force and equipment in place to support the level of sales. Also, they needed to forecast certain individual components, and we'll see how that's done in the next chapter when we talk about planning bills of material.

The Law of Large Numbers

The law of large numbers states that a series of big numbers will tend to be more stable, less jumpy, less "nervous" — and thus easier to forecast than small ones. Have you ever noticed how the sales forecast for the entire company is usually pretty accurate? And that individual item forecasts are often all over the place? This is the law of large numbers at work, and it represents another good way to reduce forecast error.

That's part of what happened with Company D's forecasts of valve sales. Let's recap their experience:

- First, they significantly reduced the numbers of items they had to forecast. Fewer forecasts mean less forecast error.

- Second, the remaining forecasts were not at the detailed, end item level but rather were aggregated numbers covering product families and models. This is where the law of large numbers kicked in: Larger numbers mean less forecast error.

Ultimately, Company D forecasted much less, and at the same time had much less forecast error. It sounds like a free lunch, too good to be true, but there are parallels elsewhere. One is from the world of quality. Thirty years ago just about everyone believed that increasing quality increases cost. "You want higher quality? You'll have to tighten specifications, hire more inspectors, pay more for purchased items, and on and on. All of this will raise your costs. You'll have to decide how much quality you can afford."

Today we know that's not true. Now we know that higher quality leads to *lower* costs, not higher.

There's a similar example in the area of on-time shipping performance. The conventional wisdom says: "You want to do a better job of shipping on time and having fewer backorders? Well you'll have to increase finished goods inventory, maybe by a lot. You'll have to decide how much customer service you can afford." Companies today are learning that's not true either. Through Lean Manufacturing techniques resulting in speed and agility and the use of planning bills, it's possible to sharply increase customer service and simultaneously reduce inventories.

And so it is with forecasting. In most cases, it's possible to forecast less, spend less time doing it, and wind up with much less forecast error. More on this important topic in the next chapter.

Gripes and Tips

Gripe: *If we could just get an accurate forecast, it would solve all our problems.*

Tip: We feel that focusing on forecast accuracy is not the best way to get better forecasts. Rather, let's look at the two principles we've seen in this chapter:

> **Principle #6: The best way to increase forecast accuracy is to focus on reducing forecast error.**

> **Principle #7: Bias is the worst kind of forecast error; strive for zero bias.**

CHAPTER 5

LEVEL

Gripe: *We need more detail in our forecasts.*

Let's consider the following question: How much forecast detail is really needed? The answer is that it depends on whom you're asking.

Charlie Owens is the CEO of Amalgamated Consolidated Enterprises (ACE), parent of the World Wide Widget Works. Ask Charlie what level of detail he needs in the forecast from World Wide, and he'll probably say something like, "Not much. I'm mostly interested in seeing division-wide projections for sales and profitability."

Now ask the same question of Paul Shaw, the production scheduler at World Wide. Paul might say, "I need total detail, by SKU, and we'd like to have that for at least the next 12 months. But so far we haven't been able to convince Marketing to give us that much."

Who's correct? Well, Charlie's right on the mark but Paul is probably asking for more than he really needs. And were he to get what he's asking for, it might not be very helpful. But it's certainly true that as a scheduler, Paul needs more detail in the forecast than Charlie the CEO.

The Forecasting Pyramid

Other people in the company would need differing levels of forecast detail. Take a look at the pyramid shown in Figure 5-1. It shows a number of levels at which the forecast could exist. Most people within the company would require more detail than Charlie, whose needs are way up at the top of the pyramid. For Operation's purposes, one set of numbers covering all of World Wide Widgets is simply not enough detail upon which to base decisions on future plant capacities, suppliers, manpower, and so on.

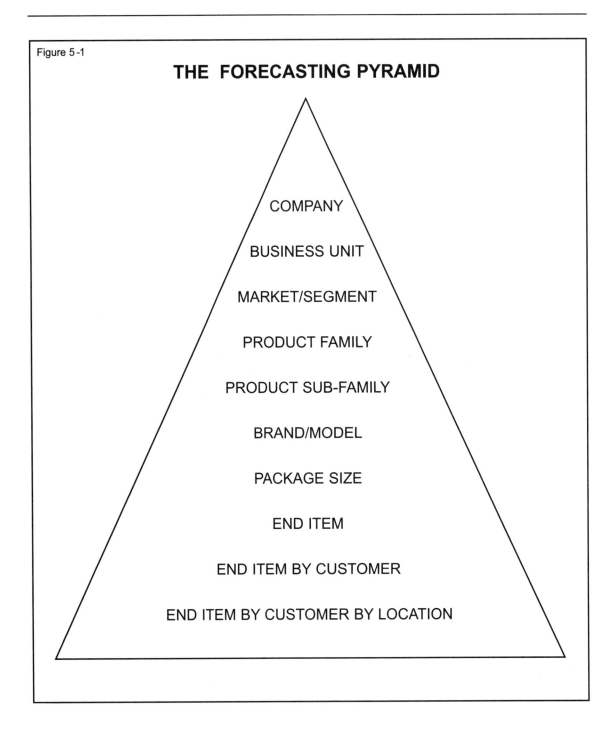

Figure 5-1

THE FORECASTING PYRAMID

COMPANY

BUSINESS UNIT

MARKET/SEGMENT

PRODUCT FAMILY

PRODUCT SUB-FAMILY

BRAND/MODEL

PACKAGE SIZE

END ITEM

END ITEM BY CUSTOMER

END ITEM BY CUSTOMER BY LOCATION

Avoid Excessive Detail

By the same token, most folks will need *less* detail than Paul is asking for (and perhaps even Paul himself is in this category). There are several problems with too much detail:

1. Forecast error will tend to be higher as the forecast numbers are chopped up into smaller and smaller pieces. Forecasting higher in the pyramid means fewer, and larger, numbers. The law of large numbers takes hold and forecast error decreases.

2. Another problem with forecasting at too low a level is that it gets people bogged down in detail. They often can't see the forest for the trees. Forecasting so many items often consumes their mental energy and diverts their focus, with the risk that they miss the bigger picture: how the models, brands, and product families are faring.

3. Lastly, too much forecasting is just a pain in the neck. It's no fun and it takes too much time. People, even those with job titles such as "forecast analyst," can almost always spend their time more profitably by not having to deal with extreme detail. Given the degree of downsizing, de-layering, and consolidation that's gone on, people in most companies really can't afford to be involved in activities that don't add value.

One company in the whiskey business learned that forecasting at the lowest possible level would be counterproductive. Were they to do that, there would simply be too much unneeded detail. For example, a case of 750 ml Old Loudmouth Bourbon going to Pennsylvania is a different stockkeeping unit from the identical product going to Ohio, because they take different case labels. While this company *stored* most of its forecasting data at a very low level, essentially end item by customer by location, it did most of its forecasting at the brand/package size level. It had good forecasting software allowing it to easily aggregate up to brand/pack size or higher.

But, you might be thinking, how does the plant know which of the two products to make? Well, until shortly before the packaging run, the plant doesn't care. The lead time to get printed case labels is one day. And they can schedule that via *the customer order*. All of the other components are common; they can do their forward planning from forecasts at the brand/pack size level or higher and not have to worry about the two, or ten, or twenty SKUs that are different only because of the case label.

There are two important concepts here:

1. The concept of common versus unique components. A large proportion of common components makes it more practical to forecast higher in the pyramid. Commonality is good. In our example, there was only one unique component: the case label.

2. The role of lead time. Short lead times also enhance opportunities to forecast higher in the pyramid. In the example, the case label's lead time was one day. Had the lead time been six months, forecasting higher up would have been far less practical.

Let's stay with this last point for just a moment. Paul Shaw, the production scheduler at our widget company, wants forecasts in end item detail for 12 months into the future. Two questions: One, does Paul need end item detail for 12 months into the future? Answer: almost certainly not. Next question: Does Paul need forecasts in end item detail for some period of time? Answer: maybe.

Let's say the lead times for all widget components are ten weeks or less. The internal manufacturing time is three weeks at most. What this means is that Paul *may* need the detail for 13 weeks into the future. But no more. Why then should Sales & Marketing be required to provide 12 months of detail, when only three months are needed? We don't think they should.

Paul, however, may come right back and say: "Wait a minute. I need that mix forecast for capacity planning purposes. I can't get my machine loads right unless I can see the mix details." Our reply: We don't think so. We recommend that Paul try using an aggregate forecast at a level that lets him see the larger mix issues, make some simplifying assumptions for the balance, use a technique called Rough-Cut Capacity Planning (see Chapter 7) to calculate the future workload, and watch the mix issue closely as it becomes visible inside the Planning Time Fence. This, we believe, will yield future capacity plans of equal or greater validity than using detail that extends far out into the future and hence is very questionable.

Sometimes folks in Accounting feel the same way as Paul. They want all that mix detail for a year or more in order to calculate costs, apply overhead, and so on. Our advice to them is the same as to Paul: Use an aggregate forecast at a level that lets you see the big mix issues, make some assumptions on the balance, and go with it. At the end of the day, you'll probably be better off, and cause a lot less work for yourselves and your colleagues in Sales & Marketing.

Now for a principle: **Forecast the volume; manage the mix. Wherever possible, forecast at higher, aggregate levels. Forecast in detail only where necessary.** It's more accurate, it's less work, and it tells you all or almost all that you need to know outside the Planning Time Fence. If you have some long lead time purchased items, forecast those at the detail level by exception. Forecast the vast majority of items in aggregate.

Figure 5-2 displays the conditions enabling the forecasting process to occur at a higher level. One of the points it makes is the shorter the lead time the better. If you're in a company with long lead times and many non-common components, you may be having a rough time if your customers want their products quickly. You're probably being required to forecast many products far into the future, and that's a hard dollar as the saying goes. It's tough to do and also it's hard to provide good customer service in such an environment. If you could shorten the lead times — at your suppliers and/or in your plants — life might get a lot easier. We'll return to this topic of reducing lead times when we talk about the "Suicide Quadrant" in Chapter 9.

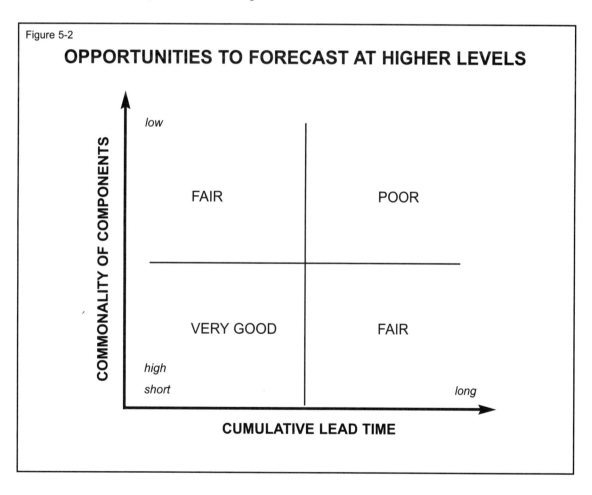

Figure 5-2

OPPORTUNITIES TO FORECAST AT HIGHER LEVELS

We'll get back to commonality of components in just a minute, when we talk about planning bills. But first, let's look at some other techniques to enable forecasting higher in the pyramid.

Roll-Up and Blow-Down

Roll-up, sometimes called aggregation, refers to combining lower level data into higher level families. It can be used to aggregate detailed history or detailed future forecasts. Blow-down, sometimes called proration, means taking a forecast at an aggregated level and chopping it into smaller pieces for the lower levels. Both of these can be useful, but be careful. Here's why.

Rolling-up detailed history into families to look at aggregate trends and patterns presents no problem. Forecasters — folks like product managers, marketing directors, vice presidents of Sales & Marketing — most often like to review forecasts at these aggregated levels rather than having to deal with large amounts of detail.

Blow-down is the flip side of the roll-up process. Frequently, forecasters will make changes to the forecast at these aggregate levels and, inside the Planning Time Fence, these changes need to be reflected in the lower level items. How does that happen? Well, blow-down can be an effective way of getting to the detail. However, some cautions in its use are in order. For example:

At World Wide Widgets, Paula Morgan (Product Manager) and Sam Mason (VP Sales & Marketing) having been talking about a happy development: One of their competitors in medium widgets has just exited the business. This competitor had substantial sales volume in the *low end* of the line, and Paula and Sam are confident they can pick up a big piece of that. They're estimating that overall sales of medium widgets will increase by about 5 percent. Question: Should they put the 5 percent increase into the forecast for medium widgets and then have the forecasting software blow it down to all of the products in that family? No, they shouldn't. The reason is that the sales increase will not be evenly distributed over all medium widgets, but rather will be concentrated in the low end. Thus, they should specify which products will be impacted and allow the software to prorate the increase only into those.

Another example: Some time later, Sam and Paula decide to take a price increase on large widgets. The increase will apply to all large widgets, and it's expected to decrease overall sales by about 2 percent for the next six months. In this case, it's probably okay to have the software automatically prorate the decrease across all products in this family (unless they feel that a specific widget or group of them will be more, or less, affected).

The message here: Given adequate software, blowing-down is easy but should be done with caution to ensure that the new aggregated forecast is prorated properly. Often, human intervention by individual end item is required to ensure that this happens.

We believe that you need not spend time doing and reconciling this blow-down process *outside* the Planning Time Fence where the detail isn't necessary. In that time zone, the aggregate forecasts are used to generate rough-cut plans. The detail would most likely be unnecessary, potentially inaccurate, time consuming, and confusing.

Good forecasting software can be a real asset here. We believe that, for many companies, good aggregation and proration capabilities within the forecasting software are more important than the software's statistical forecasting formulas.

Store Low

As we said earlier, it's better not to forecast at the lowest level possible. Higher will almost always be better. On the other hand, it's best to *store* the actual data at a very low level, which in some companies means storing by stockkeeping unit by customer by location. That makes it possible to capture and retain very specific demand for certain customers and to view it when necessary. In addition, storing *forecast* data at a low level can help a lot with promotions.

In the example of the whiskey company, let's say that the state of Ohio, which has state-run liquor stores, had decided to have an aggressive promotion on 750 ml Old Loudmouth Bourbon from April through June; they anticipate that sales will be 300 percent of normal during that period. It's important to get that kind of intelligence into your formal forecasting system on a rigorous and managed basis. Being able to store forecasts at a very detailed level and then roll them up into meaningful groupings makes that possible. That in turn can make forecasting more effective and, dare we say, more fun.

Exceptions

Sometimes it's necessary to make detailed, mix forecasts farther out into the future. Here are several examples.

Company L makes products with a highly seasonal sales curve and has the following issues to contend with:

- Eighty percent of their annual sales volume is tied to Christmas.

- They ship almost all of that volume during September, October, and November.

- They don't have enough capacity to produce that much volume in that period. They must produce early, in order to meet their customers' demand.

- They start this early production, called the "pre-build," in the spring. To select the items to pre-build, they focus on A products (20 percent of the items; 80 percent of the volume).

At that point, for those items, the Planning Time Fence has moved out to about eight months. They must have a detailed, mix forecast for the items to be pre-built covering that eight-month or more period. Do keep in mind, however, that they don't need mix forecasts for all their products, only *the ones to be pre-built.*

Company J makes builders' tools. Here's their situation:

- About 85 percent of their products are made in their domestic plants, which have done a fine job with Lean Manufacturing and can produce within just a few days. They do no mix forecasting for these products.

- The balance of their product line is outsourced in Asia and these carry a six-month lead time. That's the Planning Time Fence for these items and they must forecast the mix for that 15 percent of the business for six months out.

We feel that Company J needs to ask itself a question: Why do the Asian plants need a six-month lead time? Why can't they produce product within just a few days, like the U.S. plants? Yes there is shipping time, which might be about a month. Add that to, say, a one-week production time and throw in another week for consolidation of shipments and so forth. What we have is a six-*week* lead time, not six months. This means less detailed forecasting, better customer service, lower inventories, and more responsiveness to shifts in customer demand.

Planning Bills of Material

First, let's dissect this phrase. "Planning" means that this is a technique used in future planning. The term "bills of material"[1] refers to a grouping of the components necessary to make a product. However — and here's the tricky part — planning bills are not producible; you can't make anything directly from a planning bill. They exist solely for planning purposes, so that material and capacity can be available when the customer order arrives.

Small consumer widgets is one of the product families at World Wide. Each product in this make-to-order family contains a base unit, a control module, a power supply, a sensor, and packaging. The base unit is standard across all models of small consumer widgets, while the other components vary from product to product, as follows:

Control Module	5 options
Sensor	4 options
Power Supply	3 options
Packaging	20 variations (depending on product configuration, private brand customer, and so on)
Base Unit	standard

Figure 5-3 shows this arrangement graphically.

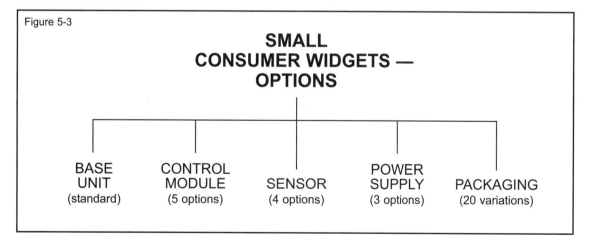

Figure 5-3

SMALL CONSUMER WIDGETS — OPTIONS

| BASE UNIT (standard) | CONTROL MODULE (5 options) | SENSOR (4 options) | POWER SUPPLY (3 options) | PACKAGING (20 variations) |

---

[1] Other terms for bills of material include formulas, recipes, or ingredients list.

Given this array of options, the possible number of models within small consumer widgets is 1,200 (5 control modules *times* 4 sensors *times* 3 power supplies *times* 20 packaging variations *times* 1 base unit). This means potentially 1,200 end items to forecast. This will be particularly challenging when one considers that the annual sales for this entire product family are about 8,500 units per month (less than 8 per possible model). The law of large numbers is definitely not at work here.

World Wide should consider setting up a planning bill for this product family. This is an arrangement that will show each option and its projected frequency of being ordered by customers. In Figure 5-4, we can see that the base unit has a forecasted frequency of 100 percent. This makes sense, because there is only one base unit; it's standard and every customer order for small consumer widgets will need one of them.

On the other hand, the five control module options are shown along with their forecasted frequency of order, expressed as a percentage. Ditto for the other options. Keep in mind that these percentages are truly forecasts, i.e., projections of customer orders for these optional items. Most companies derive these primarily from past history, with adjustments for new options, changing customer preferences, pricing, and so forth.

So, if World Wide were to use a planning bill, how many possible end items would they need to forecast? Answer: only 33 (5 control modules *plus* 4 sensors *plus* 3 power supplies *plus* 20 packaging variations *plus* 1 base unit[2]). Thirty-three is a far cry from 1,200. This will take advantage of the law of large numbers, thus making forecasting easier and, at the same time, sharply reducing forecast error. Better results for less effort.

Companies using the process called Sales & Operations Planning (see Chapter 6) would generate a forecast for the product family. (In our example, small consumer widgets. This would be the same as the forecast for the base unit, because of the one-to-one relationship.) This forecast would be authorized or modified by top management and would then be "exploded" against the option percentages for each component to create requirements for these components.

---

[2] In actual practice, companies often take all of the common parts from the option components and group them together into what's called a "common parts bill." For example, let's say every sensor option uses the same housing. That housing could be pulled from the sensor bills of material and placed with the base unit, carrying a usage of 100 percent. Common parts bills reduce uncertainty, at the cost of some added complexity. For additional information on this topic, see John F. Proud, *Master Scheduling, Second Edition* (1999). New York: John Wiley & Sons, pp. 182–192, 278–284.

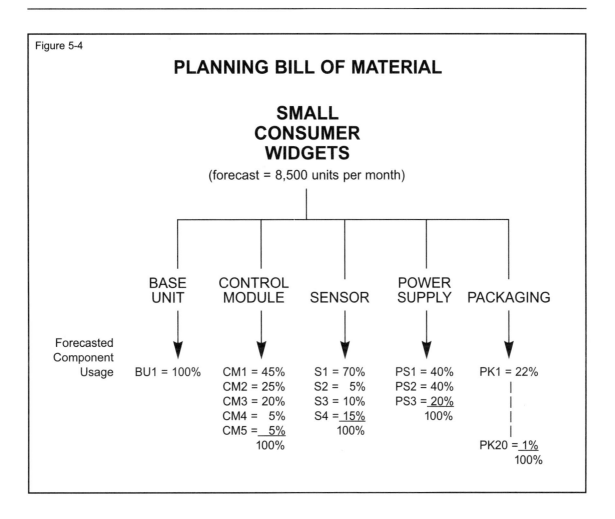

Figure 5-4

PLANNING BILL OF MATERIAL

SMALL CONSUMER WIDGETS

(forecast = 8,500 units per month)

	BASE UNIT	CONTROL MODULE	SENSOR	POWER SUPPLY	PACKAGING
Forecasted Component Usage	BU1 = 100%	CM1 = 45%	S1 = 70%	PS1 = 40%	PK1 = 22%
		CM2 = 25%	S2 = 5%	PS2 = 40%	
		CM3 = 20%	S3 = 10%	PS3 = 20%	
		CM4 = 5%	S4 = 15%	100%	
		CM5 = 5%	100%		PK20 = 1%
		100%			100%

You may be wondering how anything gets built, because you sure can't build the planning bill. Well, when the customer order arrives, there is certainty as to what is needed. We know which components they're ordering. At that point, a "live" bill of material is created for this specific order and that's what gets built. It might look like this:

Customer Order #:	13579	
Product Type:	Medium Consumer Widget	
Quantity :	100	
Components:	Control module:	CM3
	Sensor:	S1
	Power supply:	PS3
	Packaging	PK14

Please note that there is no top-level part number here. That function is served by the customer order number. It goes into the computer with a quantity of 100, in this example, and the components are linked to it via bill of material type records.

Simultaneously, the planning bill quantities are reduced accordingly, to avoid duplicating demand. What has happened, therefore, is that uncertainty (in the form of the planning bill) has been replaced by the certainty of the customer order.

This approach also works for make-to-stock products, the main difference being that the live bill of material is created *prior* to receipt of customer orders, triggered most often by the need to replenish the finished goods inventory — typically on those products with high volumes that the company has decided to stock for immediate shipment, while treating the ones with lower volume as finished to order.

Some of you might be wondering about the incoming order rate given that it might not be level from day to day. Successful users of this planning bill technique frequently will designate one or several very high-volume SKUs as the buffer. When incoming orders are low, they'll make buffer product and put it into inventory. Then, on days when orders are high, they can make all non-buffer product and draw down the buffer inventory on the high volume product(s).

A word about lead time: In the last chapter we talked about speed and agility helping to reduce the need to forecast. Whether you'll be adopting this planning bill approach or not, we urge you to address the speed and agility issue on the plant floor and in Purchasing. Long lead times are bad. They increase inventories, costs, and confusion; they decrease customer service, flexibility, and finger pointing. Our colleague Dick Ling says it best: "Long lead times are our natural enemy."

Deciding Where to Forecast

We'd love to be able to give you a formula that will tell you at which level to forecast. Unfortunately, we don't know of one. However, we can give you some thoughts and also some questions to help you decide. First the thoughts:

1. Keep in mind the distinction between the forecast itself, as it resides in the computer, and the ways in which it can be viewed. Ron White, a senior partner with Caseware/Demand Solutions, says it well: "One forecast, many views." How the forecast is stored and maintained is one thing; displaying it to a variety of different users is a separate — and much easier — issue, given adequate software.

2. Don't forget about Pareto's Law, the 80/20 approach[3]. Within a given family of products, some of the higher volume SKUs might be forecasted individually, even by customer and location as is often the case for products going to mass merchandisers. The remaining products in the family might be grouped together and forecasted at a higher level, perhaps by model, by brand, or by sub-family.

Now for the questions:

1. What do the other departments — Operations, Finance, Distribution, and so forth — really need? How much detail and in which parts of the overall forecast horizon? Will the proposed approach be able to satisfy their needs?

2. Who does the forecasting? Not "who uses the forecast" but rather, who *does* it? Concentrate on these people and their needs. In what terms do they usually think? What will they be comfortable with?

3. How is the forecasting done? For example, will the field sales force be involved in setting the forecast? That implies that much of the forecasting work will need to be done with a customer view. This could be at a very low level as we've seen (end item by customer) or perhaps at a higher level (model, brand, etc.) aggregated for each customer.

Gripes and Tips

Gripe: *We need more detail in our forecasts.* Our response: Maybe, but probably not. If you're talking about forecasting in detail out beyond your Planning Time Fence, we think you should reconsider, for the reasons we've covered in this chapter.

> **Principle# 8: Forecast the volume; manage the mix.**
> **Wherever possible forecast at higher, aggregate levels.**
> **Forecast in detail only where necessary.**

---

[3] This refers to what's been called the "vital few and trivial many." It states that in a given group of items, about 80 percent of the impact comes from about 20 percent of the items.

CHAPTER 6

USES

Gripe: *Forecasting is a waste of time around here;*
nobody ever reads them.

Our topic here: Where does the forecast go and what does it do when it gets there? Back in Chapter 1, we touched on the uses of the forecast and we saw a list dealing with that subject (repeated here as Figure 6-1).

Figure 6-1

USES FOR FORECASTS

Use	Unit of Measure	Forecast Horizon
Financial planning	Dollars	Current and future fiscal years
Sales planning	Units/dollars	Weeks, months, quarters
Capacity planning	Units/hours	Months, quarters, years
Advanced procurement	Units	Weeks, months, quarters
Master scheduling	Units	Weeks, months

To put it another way, the forecast feeds the planning functions for finance, sales force staffing and activities, production capacity, supplier capacity and commitment, and is often a direct input into the master production schedule. Let's look at these elements one by one.

Financial Planning

The forecast of future sales is, of course, essential for this function. It affects financial planning in primarily three ways:

1. The longer range portion of the Business Plan. Sometimes called the "out years," this is the part of the business plan that begins with Year 2 in the future and may extend out to Year 5 or more.

2. The first year of the Business Plan, i.e., the annual budget.

3. Changes to the annual budget.

As we saw in Figure 6-1, these forecasts are typically in dollars. Once per year they go into a budgeting cycle which includes setting future production volumes. This is necessary in order to determine production rates, which are needed to nail down overhead absorption. This of course is necessary to determine product cost, which is used for determining profit and loss, inventory valuation, and more.

The preparation of the sales forecast for business planning and budgeting purposes is seen in many companies as a lot of work, very time consuming, and a major pain in the neck. For those of you who feel that way, we may have some good news for you in just a bit, when we talk about Sales & Operations Planning. Stay tuned.

Sales Planning

There are two primary sets of resources involved in getting orders from customers and getting them shipped: resources on the demand (Sales & Marketing) side and those related to supply[1]. Sales Planning is the function of assuring that the forecast is attainable with the resources on the Sales & Marketing side. Examples of the issues it addresses include:

- Do we have, or can we add, enough salespeople (both in the field and in the office) to obtain the volume of orders that the forecast is calling for? If not, we have made a bad forecast.

- Will the necessary sales promotion materials (displays, literature, advertising, etc.) be available to get the forecasted volume of orders? If not, we've made a bad forecast.

- Do we have enough resources to deliver the necessary training (on new products, new applications, etc.) to hit the forecast? If not, we've made a bad forecast.

---

[1] Regarding the latter, production resources are addressed via Rough-Cut Capacity Planning. A similar technique for suppliers is sometimes referred to as "Rough-Cut Material Planning."

- If we're answering "yes" to these kinds of questions, then the next issue is this: Do the "yesses" apply to all sales districts/territories/regions or are there some that are coming up short? If so, will the problem prevent the forecast from being realized? If so, we need to either make plans to solve the discrepancies or to lower the forecast. If we don't do one or another, we've made a bad forecast.

Sales Planning is a particularly important function in companies experiencing high growth and/or introducing a large number of new products. In all companies, however, it's essential to make the internal assumptions that surround the forecast — primarily the availability of Sales & Marketing resources — to be true and valid. The mission of Sales Planning is to do just that.

Demand and Supply

Before we get into the specifics of the remaining functions, capacity planning, advanced procurement planning, and master production scheduling, let's take a moment and review some fundamentals.

The forecast is an estimate of future demand. And, as we learned in Economics 101, demand is only half of the equation; the other half is supply. Demand represents what the customers and others want; supply refers to the resources by which those demands will be met. Thus the forecast of future demand is the key input into the development of future plans for *supply.*

It's important that these plans exist in harmony with each other, that they be in balance. If the plans for future demand and supply are not in balance, then it's extremely unlikely that *actual* demand and supply will be in balance when they materialize . . . and that's bad. An imbalance between demand and supply results in things like late shipments, unhappy customers, unplanned overtime, too much inventory, lengthy lead times, excess manufacturing costs, layoffs, and on and on.

Volume and Mix

There are two other elements we need to look at: volume and mix. The difference between these two elements might not be as clear as the distinction between demand and supply. Let's contrast them:

- Volume is the big picture; mix is the details.

- Volume deals with aggregate groupings; mix is involved with individual items and customer orders.

- Volume addresses how much; mix is more focused on which ones.

The forecast *must* feed the function of volume planning — for manpower, equipment, inventories, cash, and so on. In many companies, the forecast is also needed for planning mix. Now let's bring together these four elements: demand and supply, volume and mix.

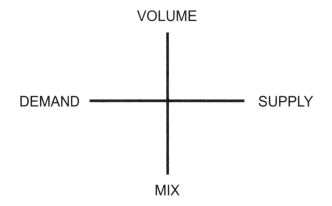

Demand and supply must be balanced at both the volume and the mix levels — or the results will be unhappy customers, layoffs, too much inventory, and on and on.

Here's a question for you: How often does your company formally plan volumes? How often do you sit down and relate future demand to future supply to ensure that the company has the necessary resources to handle this demand? If you answered once per year, you're right at the national average. This is part of the annual budgeting cycle we just talked about. The problem is that, for virtually all companies, the volume picture changes more frequently than once per year. Looking at that picture only once per year is not the best way to run the business. Let's look at a better way.

The Resource Planning Model

Figure 6-2 shows a schematic of what we call Resource Planning. If you're thinking Enterprise Resource Planning (ERP) as you read those words, fine. What this represents is a set of tools — business processes — that helps people to deal with the four fundamentals: demand and supply, volume and mix.

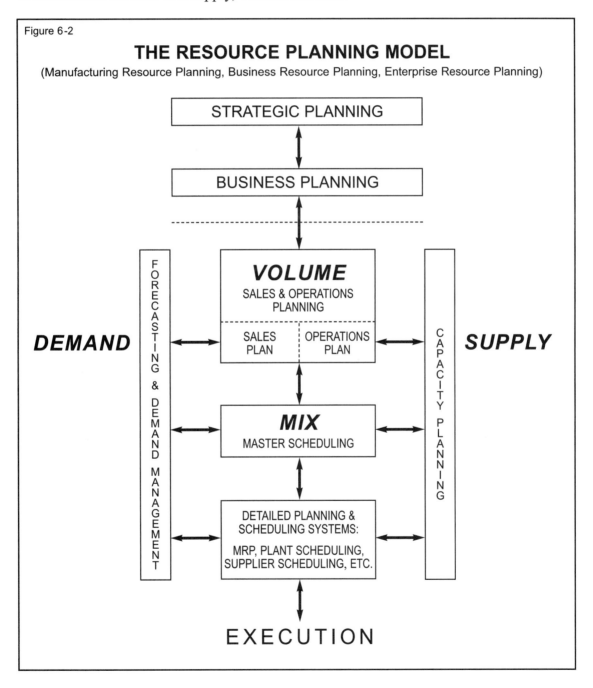

Figure 6-2

THE RESOURCE PLANNING MODEL
(Manufacturing Resource Planning, Business Resource Planning, Enterprise Resource Planning)

On the diagram, we can see these four fundamentals shown with the specific business process that addresses it. For example, the tool to balance demand and supply at the *volume level* is Sales & Operations Planning (S&OP). We can see further that, on the demand side, Forecasting and Demand Management is a primary feeder into S&OP, as is Capacity Planning for supply. Similarly, the Master Schedule is the tool used to balance demand and supply at the *mix* level.

Important attributes of this resource planning approach include the following.

- It consists of a series of business functions, all linked together.

- It is a "closed-loop" process. Note that the arrows go in both directions. This means that it has two-way communication: There is provision for feedback from the execution step and the more specific planning functions back into the more general.

- It functions in both units and dollars: units for the operational aspects of running the business, dollars for the financial side. The important thing here is that the *basic data* is the same[2]. This leads people to call this a "single-number system" or "running the business with one set of numbers."

- It can be used as a simulator. It's possible to pose "what-if" questions to this set of tools and to receive understandable answers, in both units and dollars. For example, what if sales were to increase by 20 percent in the Western Region? Could the California plant handle the increased volumes (units) and what would it cost to do so (dollars)? Alternatively, do the plants in both Texas and Indiana have enough capacity to run this volume and what are the cost implications of producing it there and shipping it out west?

The dotted line above S&OP is intended to show that Business Planning and Strategic Planning are not components of Resource Planning, but rather are primary drivers into it. Notice, however, that the line connecting Business Planning with Sales & Operations Planning has arrows going in both directions. Sometimes the future visibility provided by S&OP can lead to a decision to modify the Business Plan.

---

[2] Typically this data is kept in units and "translated" into dollars. For example, it's very practical to "dollarize" the inventory balances and sum them up to get the total valuation of the inventory. You can't go the other way; you can't derive the individual item balances from the aggregate dollars.

Please keep in mind: The elements contained within ERP are *business processes,* not software. There are software packages available to support ERP, and these are correctly referred to not as ERP but rather as Enterprise Software[3] (ES).

Some of you might be thinking: "Wait a minute. Our company doesn't have any of this ERP stuff or ES software. Is there any reason for us to get better forecasts?" Your authors' answer: There certainly is. Look at Figure 6-2 one more time. Most of the functions shown in that diagram are being done by most companies. Let's take a look:

- STRATEGIC PLANNING: Most companies do this.

- BUSINESS PLANNING: Almost all companies do this.

- SALES & OPERATIONS PLANNING: Relatively few companies do this well, if at all. This is because it's a relatively new process and not well understood by most companies.

- FORECASTING: Almost all companies do this.

- DEMAND MANAGEMENT: Included here are functions such as customer order entry and promising. All companies do this.

- CAPACITY PLANNING: Almost all companies do this, but perhaps not often enough.

- MASTER SCHEDULING: This means planning and scheduling for individual products to be built. All companies do this, but many not very well.

- DETAILED PLANNING AND SCHEDULING TOOLS: A mixed bag.

The fact is that every company is doing most of these things. Some perhaps not very well, but most of these business functions are present. We need to do the annual budget, we need to have enough manpower and equipment, we need to book customer orders, we need to schedule production, we need to buy materials, and so on. The question is not whether they are being done, but *how well* they're being done.

---

[3] See Thomas F. Wallace and Michael H. Kremzar, *ERP: Making It Happen,* 2001, New York: John Wiley and Sons, and Thomas H. Davenport, *Mission Critical,* 2000, Boston MA: Harvard Business School Press.

So, in answer to the question "will better forecasts help us if we don't have ERP?", our response is a strong, definite "yes." It will help you make better use of your existing tools. Then, when the day comes that you adopt the full ERP approach, your improved forecasts will make things run even better[4].

On the other hand, you may have most or all of ERP operating within your company. Therefore, we'd like now to examine how the forecast interacts with ERP's individual elements.

Sales & Operations Planning

As we said earlier, S&OP is a tool for balancing demand and supply at the volume level. Volume means aggregate. Therefore the forecast for S&OP must be some kind of aggregate grouping, typically by product family or sub-family. An example of a product family might be medium consumer widgets and sub-families within that could be medium consumer widgets/hydraulic and medium consumer widgets/pneumatic.

Please note: The forecast does not have to be *developed* at this level (even though it indeed might be best to do so). Many companies develop their forecasts at a lower level and then roll them up to the level required for S&OP. For example, the whiskey company we saw earlier forecasted at the brand/pack size level: Old Loudmouth Bourbon, 750 ml. This was part of the product sub-family called premium bourbons, which in turn was in the overall bourbon family.

The question arises: "What happens to the forecast after it goes into S&OP?" Figure 6-3 shows a series of steps, the first two of which — Data Gathering and Demand Planning Phase — deal directly with forecasting. They include the tasks shown earlier in Figure 3-6: Data Gathering and Preparation, Forecast Generation, Applying Judgment, Documenting Assumptions, and Decision-Making and Authorization.

From there, the monthly S&OP process moves to a Supply Planning phase, which receives the authorized forecast from the Demand Planning phase and sets the initial balance between demand and supply.

Next comes the Pre-SOP meeting, which includes key operating-level people. They develop plans and recommendations for the Executive S&OP meeting, which includes top management up to and including the president (general manager, CEO, managing director). Output from this session is the authorized company-wide game plan.

---

[4] Good ERP implementations frequently include improvement of forecasting processes.

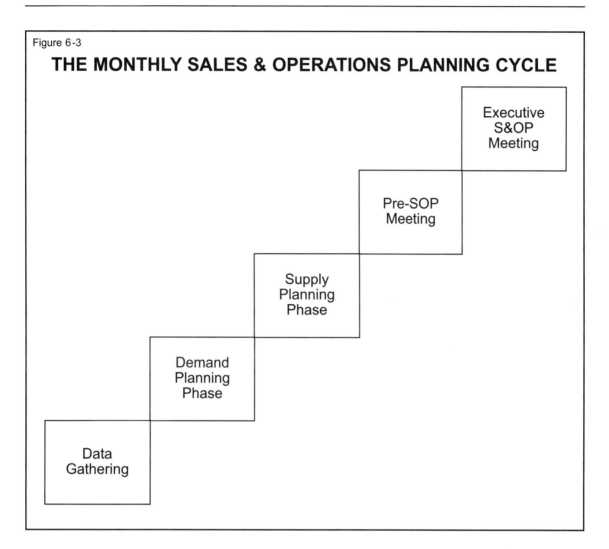

Figure 6-3

THE MONTHLY SALES & OPERATIONS PLANNING CYCLE

A sample S&OP spreadsheet is shown in Figure 6-4. One can see the forecast row near the top of the page including forecasts from prior months. These are compared to actual demand for that period and the difference is shown. On the right side of the forecast line, totals are taken for the next rolling 12 months and for the current fiscal year. (The current fiscal year total is calculated by adding actual sales year-to-date plus forecasts for the remaining months of the year.) This fiscal year total appears next to a comparable number from the Business Plan, and the difference is shown.

Let's sum up our discussion of S&OP. It has the following characteristics:
- It helps people balance demand and supply at the aggregate, volume level.
- It's a monthly process.
- It requires estimates of future demand, i.e., forecasts.
- It operates in both units and dollars.
- It involves top management and key operating level people.

Back in Chapter 3, we talked about inputs to the forecasting process, one of which is the management directive — a mandated forecast coming from the corner office. S&OP directly involves the executive staff, up to and including the president, and thus it can often help with this issue. If an aggressive forecast is not being realized, if actual sales are consistently below the forecast, and if bias is present and growing, it will be very, very visible. In fact, it will be almost impossible to ignore. The Executive S&OP meeting should be the forum to address why the forecast is not being achieved, what additional steps might be put in place to increase sales up to the forecasted level, or — worst case — to revise the forecast downward and then start looking at expense reduction so that the bottom line number is achieved. (The same point applies to a forecast that was consistently biased in the other direction — toward the low side.)

Figure 6-4

THE ACME WIDGET COMPANY – SALES & OPERATIONS PLAN FOR OCT 2001

FAMILY: MEDIUM WIDGETS (MAKE-TO-STOCK)   UNIT OF MEASURE: 1000 UNITS
TARGET LINE FILL: 99%   TARGET FIN INV: 10 DAYS ON HAND

SALES	J	A	S	O	N	D	J	F	M	3rd 3 MOS	4th 3 MOS	NEXT 12 MOS	FISCAL YEAR LATEST CALL	BUSINESS PLAN
NEW FORECAST	200	200	200	210	210	220	220	220	220	690	690	2670	$25,540	$25,400
ACTUAL SALES	222	195	227											
DIFF: MONTH	22	-5	27											
CUM		17	44											

OPERATIONS														
NEW PLAN	200	200	200	210	220	230	230	230	230	695	690	2735		
ACTUAL	200	206	199											
DIFF: MONTH	0	6	-1											
CUM		6	5											

INVENTORY														
PLAN	100	100	100	60	70	80	90	100	110	115	115			
ACTUAL	78	89	61											
DAYS ON HAND	8	9	6	6	6	7	8	9	10	10	9			
LINE FILL %	97%	98%	89%											

DEMAND ISSUES AND ASSUMPTIONS
1. FORECAST REFLECTS LAUNCH OF NEW
   DESIGNER WIDGET LINE IN 3RD QTR.

2. ASIA FORECASTED TO REACH 1999 VOLUME

SUPPLY ISSUES
1. XMAS FULL PLANT SHUTDOWN RESCHEDULED TO
   STAGGERED PARTIALS THRU FALL AND WINTER

Earlier in this chapter, we pointed out that many people actively dislike the annual budgeting process. Well, companies doing a good job with Sales & Operations Planning have found that it makes the financial planning job a lot easier. That's because S&OP deals with both units and dollars. The dollar view of the Sales & Operations Plan, which projects out for 15 or 24 or more months into the future, can be used as a primary input to preparing the Business Plan. It contains dollarized sales projections, production volumes, and finished goods inventory levels. All or most of these are essential for financial planning and typically are among the hardest items to get. With S&OP, they already exist and are updated each month. One CEO we know stated that one of the main reasons they were implementing S&OP was "to minimize the amount of time we spend on the budget. We can't afford to have our key people tied up for long time periods doing the budget."

For a complete treatment of S&OP, refer to Thomas F. Wallace, *Sales & Operations Planning — The How-To Handbook,* 1999, Cincinnati OH: T. F. Wallace & Company.

Master Scheduling

The forecast used in the Sales & Operations Planning process, after any changes in S&OP, is the same one that will go into Master Scheduling (after any modifications made in S&OP). However, it will probably *look different*, carrying more detail and going out only to the Planning Time Fence. This is because the mission of the Master Schedule is to balance demand and supply at the *mix* level. Therefore the forecast going into the Master Schedule will need to:

- be expressed in terms of individual products, SKUs, and/or customer orders , or

- permit the Master Schedule to derive schedules for individual items.

This last sentence refers primarily to planning bills. As we saw in Chapter 5, Figure 5-4, there are really two very different types of forecasts involved with planning bills. One is the volume forecast of demand for the entire family or model: medium consumer widgets, 8,500 per month (coming right out of S&OP). The other type of forecast is in percentages: it's the forecasted component usage — CM1 = 45%, CM2 = 25%, etc.

For companies not using planning bills, the forecast going into the Master Schedule is most often expressed in individual items: products, SKUs, customer orders, etc.

A simplified Master Schedule display is shown in Figure 6-5, and we'll get into the specifics of it in the next chapter. For now, please note that here also, as with S&OP, the forecast is shown near the top of the page. However, unlike the S&OP display, the near-term time periods are in weeks, not months. This is essential. Monthly time slices are simply too broad to handle effective planning for mix.

Figure 6-5

ITEM NUMBER: _____

Weeks	Past Due	1	2	3	4	5	6	7	8
Forecast									
Customer Orders (Sched.)									
Warehouse Demand									
Dependent Demand									
Inter Plant Demand									
TOTAL DEMAND									
Projected Available Balance									
Available to Promise									
Master Production Schedule									

If the Master Schedule is expressed in months, then the requirements that it sends to the downstream processes — Material Requirements Planning, Supplier Scheduling, Plant Scheduling — will also be in monthly lumps. These downstream tools will be unable to discriminate when within the month the items will be needed. Users will find that the tools within the "formal system" are not helping them, and they will revert back to the "informal system" — lots of expediting, shortage lists, red tags, and so forth.

Right now some of you might be thinking: Wait a minute, you guys! You've been telling us to use only one forecast throughout the company. But here you're telling us to use a monthly forecast for S&OP and a weekly one for the Master Schedule. What gives?

Well, the way most companies do this is to simply take the monthly forecast for each item and "chop it up" into weeks. Some companies do this very simply; they're on a 4-week/ 4-week/5-week accounting cycle, so the first two monthly forecasts of the quarter get divided by four and the last month by five. Other companies, operating on more of a calendar month cycle, divide the monthly forecast by 4.3 which approximates the number of weeks in a month. Some companies, based on their experience, will weight certain weeks of the month more heavily based on their customers' buying patterns.

In summary, we can say that an effective master scheduling process has the following characteristics:

- It balances demand and supply at the mix level — individual items.

- It reflects a valid, buildable plan. It does not ask for more production than the plants are capable of producing. The technique for this is known as Rough-Cut Capacity Planning.

- In the near- to medium-term, it's expressed in weekly — or even daily — time periods.

And, as we'll see in the next chapter, it is the source for promising customer orders validly and dependably.

Distribution Center Replenishment

Companies whose products flow through distribution centers (DCs) have a unique problem. They must worry about balancing demand and supply not only at their plants and master warehouses; they need to do the same thing at their DCs.

Distribution Requirements Planning (DRP) is an effective and widely-used tool for this[5]. The supply is normally provided from a central point such as a plant or master warehouse. Demand comes in the form of customer orders in the near term, and is forecasted farther out.

That means that the detailed forecasts will need to be expressed by *distribution center*, and extended out to the Planning Time Fence. And that's not particularly good news, because it's going in the opposite direction from the law of large numbers. For example, an item with annual unit sales of around 12,000 stocked in four DCs requires four sets of forecasts averaging 3,000 per year, 250 per month. These are small numbers, not large ones. This puts even more pressure on having good forecasting processes in place.

---

[5] Another widely used tool is the order-point method. Like any other replenishment system, it uses an estimate of future demand (a forecast) over the replenishment lead time. However, the forecast in the order-point approach is almost always based totally on past history and does not reflect anticipated changing conditions such a promotions, seasonality, price changes, etc. Furthermore, since it is not time-phased into the future, it offers little forward visibility to the Master Scheduling function.

The forecasts for DCs should come from the same source as all the rest of the forecasts. Remember Ron White's advice in the prior chapter: One forecast, many views. A good forecasting software package can be a big help here also. It can blow-down nationwide forecasts for individual products into forecasts for those products by each distribution center where they're stocked or, alternatively, to forecast individual items by distribution center if that's more appropriate.

Accessories, Supply Items, and Service Parts

These items are parts of products or are used in conjunction with products. They can be very important to some companies: highly profitable, often with margins far higher than their parent products[6], and frequently quite a lot is riding on them in terms of customer satisfaction and good will.

The bad news is that, in some cases, they can present significant forecasting challenges and can be difficult items on which to provide good customer service. (On the other hand, sometimes they behave much like the end products to which they're tied.) Let's look at them one at a time.

Accessories

Consider the example of a docking station for a laptop computer. This item is very much like a finished product: It has a number of components; it comes in a unique set of packaging; it may be displayed in retail stores. The major difference is that its future demand will be tied very closely to the demand for its parent product, the laptop.

Forecasting for items like this frequently looks a lot like the planning bill approach we saw in Chapter 5. The "dependent" item, in this case the docking station, might be forecasted to sell at a given percentage of the laptop, say 20 percent. The logic is that virtually all sales for docking stations will occur because of the laptop purchase (lost or damaged docking stations are rare) and that about one out of five laptop buyers will buy the docking station.

The law of large numbers is not working for us here, because most accessories behave like our docking station example: They sell less than the primary products they complement. Now let's look at a case where the reverse is true.

---

[6] One of the things we've learned from Activity Based Costing is that the ultra high margins on service items are sometimes not real; they're overstated by conventional accounting methods. The fact remains that many service items are highly profitable.

Supply Items

A good example here is printer cartridges. H-P, Lexmark, and others sell a lot more cartridges than they do printers. However, the future sales for these items remain tied closely to their parent products.

Forecasting for supply items usually takes a different approach from what we just saw for accessories: The driver is not sales of the parent product, but rather its *installed base*. It figures, doesn't it? What will determine future sales of print cartridges for Lexmark Z53 printers is not directly how many printers will be sold in the coming periods, but how many Z53s will be out there in use. Estimates of the total installed base of Z53s, along with usage data (the number of cartridges a typical printer uses over time) would form the basis for the cartridge forecast.

Now it's time to look at what's usually the toughest one to forecast.

Service Parts

These items, also called "spares" or "repair parts," are often the most difficult forecasting job of all. But not always. In some cases, a given service part might have reasonably high volumes, in which case it would behave much like a typical product and not pose a difficult forecasting problem. In these cases, they sometimes behave a lot like supply items in that their volumes reflect the installed base of products in the field.

Frequently, however, service parts are very low volume items, and are characterized by what's called "irregular demand" or "lumpy demand." It's not easy to give good customer service on these items, even with a lot of safety stock. Here's an example of irregular demand:

Monthly Demand 0 1 0 0 0 1 0 1 0

What makes this tough is trying to predict, not the magnitude of the demand, but rather its timing — when the demand will occur. The large number of zeros can cause problems for most statistical forecasting models, because they are designed to assume that the data is in a normal, bell-shaped curve. Not so in this case.

Lumpy demand, as opposed to merely irregular, presents an even tougher problem. Here's an example:

Monthly Demand 0 5 0 0 0 2 0 9 0

So what's the demand going to be for next month? Good luck. Some people might say to use safety stock. The problem is that, to give high customer service, we'd have had to carry nine units in stock *all year long* — and nine units is over half of the last 12 months' sales. Expensive[7].

Some interesting approaches to forecasting irregular and lumpy demand have been developed. A detailed discussion of them is beyond the scope of this book, so we've listed some sources in Appendix B. We'd like to take a different approach and think a bit outside the traditional forecasting box. Some other approaches that might help with these irregular and lumpy items include:

- Lead Time Reduction. If the replenishment lead time for these items could be reduced to less than the order fulfillment time, then as we've seen before, the need for detailed forecasting goes away. Volume forecasting will almost always be necessary, but that's a lot easier, what with the law of large numbers and all. Now in many environments, this approach just isn't possible, but it is *possible in some cases*. If you have a service parts forecasting problem, we strongly suggest that you investigate reducing lead times.

- Dedicated Facilities. Many companies have a service parts problem because these items compete for priority with parts needed for production. A common result is long lead times for service parts, a heavy dependence on forecasts that are wildly inaccurate, and unhappy customers. Well, some of these companies have made things a lot better by creating a separate department dedicated to making service parts. Within that department are the people and equipment the necessary to make the parts from start to finish, and to do it very quickly. Here also, the result can be that the need to forecast individual service parts goes away, because they can be made within the allowable time for customer order fulfillment.

- Maintenance Schedules. Frequently a major driver for service parts demand is scheduled preventive maintenance. Some companies have had success with getting visibility into their customers' upcoming maintenance schedules, and can infer future demand from them. While this might be difficult to do with all customers, getting this kind of information for the "A" customers (20 percent of the customers, 80 percent of the volume) might be quite beneficial.

---

[7] This is with the clarity of 20-20 hindsight. Nine units in safety stock might not be enough to keep us out of trouble next year. Maybe we should play it safe and go with 12. And if sales drop a bit, then we'll be carrying about a year's worth of safety stock.

Gripes and Tips

Gripe: *Forecasting is a waste of time around here; nobody ever reads them.* In other words, nobody uses the forecasts. One reason for this is that the forecasts are not reasoned, reasonable, reviewed frequently, and do not reflect the total demand. Another is the multiplicity of forecasts that we see in many companies: Different departments have different forecasts for different purposes. One thing you can be sure of is that these different forecasts never agree.

A vice president/general manager of a major business unit at Procter & Gamble said: "Our entire business team — Marketing, Sales, Product Supply, Finance, R&D — is working more effectively now that we've stopped defending different volume estimates all month. We can pull together with a 'single number' forecast that has everyone's full support." And that leads us to:

> **Principle #9: One forecast, many views. Have only one forecast, with the ability to display it in a variety of ways for different uses.**

CHAPTER 7

MANAGING DEMAND

Gripe: *We know the forecast is going to be wrong, so why do it?*

We use the forecast to get us "in the ballpark" and to get us started. Then, as soon as possible, we use more solid information — customer orders, for example — to take the place of the forecast. This leads us to our next forecasting principle: **As soon as possible, replace the unknown with the known**. Replace the forecast with something more certain, ideally customer orders.

Degrees of Uncertainty

In some cases, however, companies don't make a transition from forecasts directly to customer orders. Rather there are intervening steps, such as quotes or bids. One definition of a forecast is that it's an order we haven't gotten yet. A formal quote is also an order we don't have yet, but one that we know a good bit about and have some increased hope that it'll come in. Quotes are less uncertain than forecasts.

Similarly, in some industries, customer commitments can play a major role. This is an expression of intent by a (typically large) customer to buy a certain amount of product in a certain time period. We see this often in highly seasonal businesses. These are better than mere forecasts, in that they are expressions of intent by the customer. They are "less unknown, less uncertain." Figure 7-1 conveys this graphically.

Figure 7-1

DEGREES OF DEMAND CERTAINTY

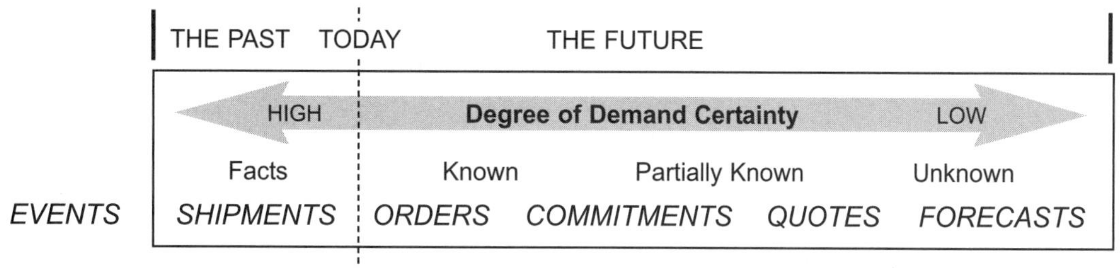

	THE PAST TODAY	THE FUTURE	
	HIGH	Degree of Demand Certainty	LOW
	Facts	Known Partially Known	Unknown
EVENTS	SHIPMENTS	ORDERS COMMITMENTS QUOTES	FORECASTS

Planning bills, as we saw, contain two kinds of forecasts: a volume forecast for the model (medium consumer widgets = 8,500 per month) and mix forecasts in the form of percentages for the options (control module, sensor, etc.). When the customer order arrives for a medium consumer widget, it specifies which control module, sensor, etc. that the customer is ordering. With this new information, we can replace the unknown, the forecast, with the known, the customer order. Let's look a bit further into this process, but with a somewhat simpler example.

Consuming the Forecast

The Northern Bleen Swivel Company (NoBS) has a line of make-to-stock products. One of these, Product # 24680, has a sales forecast of 80 per month, 20 per week[1].

Here's the picture on this item at the start of Week 1:

WEEK	1	2	3	4	5	6	7	8
SALES FORECAST	20	20	20	20	20	20	20	20

Now let's say that we book 5 customer orders on Monday and 3 on Tuesday. Here's the picture at the close of business on Tuesday.

WEEK	1	2	3	4	5	6	7	8
SALES FORECAST	12	20	20	20	20	20	20	20
CUSTOMER ORDERS	8							
TOTAL DEMAND	20	20	20	20	20	20	20	20

Notice what has happened: the 8 customer orders consumed a corresponding amount of forecast. The total demand in Week 1 is still predicted to be 20. It's important to project a stable stream of demand to the supply side (e.g. the Master Scheduling function) when that demand is stable. In this case, it almost certainly is.

Let's go forward. Week 1 is over and we have received 18 customer orders. The question now is: What is the forecast for Week 2? If you said 20, try again. To see why 20 is not the correct answer, let's look at the picture after Week 1 and focus on the first four weeks:

---

[1] NoBS is on a four-week accounting month, with 13 of them per year. If they were using conventional calendar months, they would need to divide the monthly forecast by 4.3 instead of 4.0.

WEEK	1	2	3	4	4-WEEK TOTAL
SALES FORECAST		20	20	20	
CUSTOMER ORDERS	18				
TOTAL DEMAND	18	20	20	20	78

Has the forecast changed? Yes. Please note that the total of the total demand line is now 78 rather than 80. In effect, the estimate of demand for the month, i.e., the forecast, has changed because we sold only 18 in Week 1 rather than 20.

Is that a good reason to change the forecast? We don't think so. Keep in mind that the forecast of 20 for Week 1 came about merely by dividing the month's forecast of 80 by 4. Nobody ever said that for sure we're going to sell 20 in Week 1. We merely chopped up the monthly forecast into weekly amounts to facilitate effective Master Scheduling, as we saw in the last chapter.

Actually the correct forecast for Week 2 is 22. We should roll the unsold portion of the Week 1 forecast into Week 2. Now let's see what results:

WEEK	1	2	3	4	4-WEEK TOTAL
SALES FORECAST		22	20	20	
CUSTOMER ORDERS	18				
TOTAL DEMAND	18	22	20	20	80

Our estimate of demand for the entire four-week period remains stable at 80. Let's fast forward to the end of Week 2. We sold 25 during that week, so the now the picture looks like this:

WEEK	1	2	3	4	4-WEEK TOTAL
SALES FORECAST			17	20	
CUSTOMER ORDERS	18	25			
TOTAL DEMAND	18	25	17	20	80

During the first two weeks, we have sold three more than the forecast and so we've reduced the next week's forecast to 17. Thus our forecast of demand for the month remains at 80. The stream of future demand being presented to the Master Schedule is stable, and that's important. When the Master Schedule is managed with stability, it's much easier to be flexible when it really matters: to respond to new customer orders and changes to existing ones. So, the process is to keep the forecast stable by rolling the undersold/oversold quantities during the month.

A disclaimer: As we said earlier, this is a book for people who work in companies that make things — physical products. What we're presenting here is the standard good practice for forecast consumption in manufacturing companies. However, not everyone sees it this way. Many people in the world of retailing believe that forecasting by week and reforecasting weekly is the way to go, one reason being that it helps them spot trends sooner. We have no quarrel with this, although we do wonder about the relative lack of stability that such a process might cause.

We fast forward again, this time to the end of the month. Here's the picture:

WEEK	1	2	3	4	4-WEEK TOTAL
SALES FORECAST					
CUSTOMER ORDERS	**18**	**25**	**17**	**28**	
TOTAL DEMAND	**18**	**25**	**17**	**28**	**88**

The sales forecast for the month was 80; we sold 88. Now the question is: What should we do with the oversold quantity of 8? When we were moving week-to-week, we rolled the undersold and oversold quantities into the next week. At the end of the month, however, it's not so clear. We can roll it into next month, in effect subtracting it from the 80 forecast in Month 2. Or we can drop it.

The choice revolves around this question: Does the oversold quantity represent a random forecast error or, alternatively, is it due to sales expected in Month 2 that came in early?

Most companies take the approach that, most of the time, it's random error. Thus their forecasting processes are set to drop the undersold and oversold quantities — unless overridden by a human being. The default is to drop, and the forecaster has the option of overriding the default if he or she believes that the undersold/oversold amount is not forecast error but mainly a timing issue.

A variation on this approach, as we've seen in several businesses, is to set a trigger signal, typically a percentage of the monthly forecast. As the month progresses, if the actual sales exceed the forecast plus the trigger percentage, then the item is kicked out right away for review by a human being, rather than being held to the end of the month. At month-end, of course, the full review of overages and underages takes place.

How Not to Consume the Forecast

Some people take a different approach to consuming the forecast: the greater of forecast or actual customer orders. Here's how that works:

WEEK	1	2	3	4	4-WEEK TOTAL
SALES FORECAST	20	20	20	20	
CUSTOMER ORDERS	12	24			
TOTAL DEMAND	20	24	20	20	84
PROJECTED AVAILABLE BALANCE 80	60	36	16	-4	
MASTER SCHEDULE ORDER			← 60 in week 5		

We've just increased the forecast to 84. Why? Not because of higher sales. In fact, for the first two weeks of the month we're running below forecast because our sales month-to-date are 36. This is not a problem, but on the other hand it's certainly not a reason to increase the forecast.

If we were using the greater of forecast or actual sales, the projected available balance would go negative in Week 4. This would cause the logic of the Master Scheduling program to issue recommendations to reschedule the order due in Week 5. It would recommend that it be rescheduled in to Week 4 (and it would probably issue similar recommendations for other Master Schedule orders out beyond Week 5). If the Master Scheduler did so, he or she would be creating instability and forcing unnecessary schedule changes that could be expensive and damaging to morale.

This approach is one reason why so many resource planning efforts (MRP/ERP) have not worked well. The forecast was not consumed correctly, and this caused erroneous and unstable demand data to routinely enter the Master Scheduling process.

Promising Customer Orders

A key element in shipping customer orders on time is to promise them validly. To see how to do that, we need to look at the simplified Master Schedule display for the Northern Bleen Swivel Company that follows. We can see a row for the projected available (inventory) balance, one for Available-to-Promise, and one for the Master Schedule itself.

The projected available balance row is the running sum of beginning inventory (80 in our example) minus the demand, plus the supply as represented by the Master Schedule (60 units in Week 5 and Week 8). In effect, this row is a critique of the demand/supply balance.

We are at the beginning of Week 1, and there are no customer orders for this item. Ready for a quiz? A customer calls and wants to order 27 in Week 3. Can we — validly — say yes? Some people say "no" because the projected available balance in Week 3 is down to 20. That, however, is not the correct answer. The reason is that the logic of Available-to-Promise (ATP) does not consider forecast. Forecasts are orders we haven't gotten yet. The promising of customer orders centers around relating actual demand (customer orders) to inventory. That inventory can be current (80 on hand) or future (60 in each of Weeks 5 and 8) as expressed by the Master Schedule.

NORTHERN BLEEN SWIVEL   MASTER SCHEDULE

PRODUCT #: 24680   MEDIUM CONSUMER BLEEN SWIVEL

WEEK	1	2	3	4	5	6	7	8
SALES FORECAST	20	20	20	20	20	20	20	20
CUSTOMER ORDERS								
TOTAL DEMAND	20	20	20	20	20	20	20	20
PROJECTED AVAILABLE BALANCE 80	60	40	20	0	40	20	0	40
AVAILABLE TO PROMISE	?							
MASTER SCHEDULE					60			60

The correct answer lies in the Available-to-Promise row, in which your friendly authors failed to put any data. Shame on us. Let's look at our display again, this time showing the ATP data.

PRODUCT #: 24680   MEDIUM CONSUMER BLEEN SWIVEL

WEEK	1	2	3	4	5	6	7	8
SALES FORECAST	20	20	20	20	20	20	20	20
CUSTOMER ORDERS								
TOTAL DEMAND	20	20	20	20	20	20	20	20
PROJECTED AVAILABLE BALANCE 80	60	40	20	0	40	20	0	40
AVAILABLE TO PROMISE (ATP)	80				60			60
MASTER SCHEDULE					60			60

Now the answer should be clear. Yes, we can validly promise the order for 27 in Week 3 because it fits within the Available-to-Promise of 80 in Week 1. In effect, we can reserve 27 of that 80 for this order. After we do that and book the order, our display will look like this.

PRODUCT #: 24680   MEDIUM CONSUMER BLEEN SWIVEL

WEEK	1	2	3	4	5	6	7	8
SALES FORECAST	20	13		20	20	20	20	20
CUSTOMER ORDERS			27					
TOTAL DEMAND	20	13	27	20	20	20	20	20
PROJECTED AVAILABLE BALANCE 80	60	47	20	0	40	20	0	40
AVAILABLE TO PROMISE (ATP)	53				60			60
MASTER SCHEDULE					60			60

We've booked the customer order for 27 in Week 3. Also we:

• Consumed the forecast — 20 out of Week 3, the remaining 7 out of Week 2.

• Updated the projected available balance line. Please note that the master schedule orders of 60 in Weeks 5 and 8 are still scheduled to come in when needed. This is a result of consuming the forecast properly.

• Updated the Available-to-Promise row to reflect the booked customer order.

Next quiz: A customer wants 35 in Week 5. Can we validly say yes? Absolutely. Here's how it would look after that order were booked.

PRODUCT #: 24680   MEDIUM CONSUMER BLEEN SWIVEL

WEEK	1	2	3	4	5	6	7	8
SALES FORECAST	20	13		5		20	20	20
CUSTOMER ORDERS			27		35			
TOTAL DEMAND	20	13	27	5	35	20	20	20
PROJECTED AVAILABLE BALANCE 80	60	47	20	15	40	20	0	40
AVAILABLE TO PROMISE (ATP)	53				25			60
MASTER SCHEDULE					60			60

Next case: Our best customer, the Smith Company, calls and wants 65 in Week 2. Can we do that? Well, not according to these numbers; we have only 53 available until Week 5. This is a case where the order entry software needs to kick this order out for a human being to evaluate and resolve. However, we probably don't want to say no to this very important customer. Some relevant questions are:

- Can we move up some of the 60 units master scheduled for Week 5 into Week 3? That would enable us to reallocate 12 of the 27 promised in Week 3 over to the new Smith order in Week 2 and still ship both orders complete: 65 in Week 2 and 27 in Week 3.

- If we can't change the Master Schedule (perhaps due to material or capacity constraints), does the customer with the 27 order in Week 3 need all 27 at that time? Could they take half in Week 3 and half two weeks later?

- Does Smith need all 65 in Week 2? Might it be okay with them if we ship 50 in Week 2 and the balance (15) in Week 5?

- Can we substitute another product for the one Smith wants? Do we have availability of that and will it be okay with Smith?

Please note: Available-to-Promise *does not make decisions to ship or not to ship. It does not make decisions on which customer gets product in limited supply.* Its job is to fill the demand where supply is available — now or in the future — and when that's not possible, to kick it out to *human beings for evaluation and decision making.* If you're starting to think that this is a high-communication process, you're absolutely right. Companies who do this well communicate intensively among the Master Scheduler(s), Sales, Production, Purchasing, and — where appropriate — top management.

We've been looking at an example of a make-to-stock product, but the Available-to-Promise approach works just as well for most make-to-order products. The main difference is that there's no finished inventory for those items[2].

Here are some important issues regarding Available-to-Promise:

- Most companies get orders with more than one line item. This implies that the Available-to-Promise function must check all items in the order before it can determine when that order can be shipped complete.

- In many companies, the volume of incoming orders is so large that this Available-to-Promise function is automated. This implies that the order entry function must have access to the Master Schedule and, for companies who've installed Enterprise Software (ES), this capability should be there. In a company without Enterprise Software, it may be more difficult to get this capability but it's almost always doable.

- Companies with more than one order entry point can run the risk of promising the same availability twice. For example, the order entry person in Des Moines might promise an order at 10:00 a.m., and her counterpart in Dallas might be looking at the same item at 10:30. If the data has not been updated in the interim, the guy in Dallas could inadvertently make an invalid promise. Therefore, the ATP function in environments like this needs to operate in real time, with the data being updated at the time of entry into the system.

Some customers want their orders shipped complete. Other customers want as much of their order as soon as possible and are willing to live with split shipments. Certain companies have customized their ATP process to reflect individual customer preferences. In the first case, the ATP logic would promise shipment based on availability of all items in the order. The latter case would show multiple promise dates for this order, one for each shipment as items became available.

---

[2] Another difference with make-to-order is that normally the Available-to-Promise numbers are zero within the Planning Time Fence. This time period is expected to be sold out, i.e., filled with sold orders.

Another positive development is the emergence of a technique called Capable-to-Promise. Available-to-Promise gets its future supply information solely from what's been master scheduled; Capable-to-Promise looks at that also, but goes a step further. The software asks itself the question: They don't have enough of these scheduled to meet this order, but could they make enough if they wanted to? Do they have material and capacity to do this? Or, in some cases, could they take some material and capacity that is currently committed to other scheduled products, possibly for inventory replenishment, and use that to meet this demand? Or, can the Master Schedule be rejuggled to enable this order to be promised when the customer wants it? Capable-to-Promise is powerful stuff, and can be quite helpful.

One last quiz: The Jones Company calls up and wants 70 in Week 6. Can we validly accept that order? Well, according to these numbers, we can. We can take all 25 Available-to-Promise in Week 5 and 45 out of the 53 in Week 1. But maybe . . . just maybe . . . we wouldn't want to do that. Might we want to think twice before we promise that order? Your authors think so, and that leads us to our next topic.

Abnormal Demand

Abnormal demand is hard to deal with, and few companies manage it well. In many cases, the forecast is blamed for being wildly inaccurate and thus causing big problems, when in fact the *real culprit* is the company's inability to manage abnormal demand.

Let's continue with the above example where Jones wants 70 in Week 6. This is a very large order, representing nearly one month's worth of demand but coming from a single customer. What about the other orders that we fully expect to come in during Weeks 1 through 4?

One possible scenario is that the Jones Company is the only customer for this product. If so, it's probably just fine to promise that availability to Jones. But if there are other customers taking this product, then letting Jones have this relatively large amount of product is probably not a good idea. Who are these Jones people anyhow? Are they an existing customer, one who's been with us for a while? Or is this the first time we've ever heard from them? Maybe they're coming to us because their supplier's plant had a fire and is out of commission for a while. In this case, the Jones order is quite possibly a "one-time shot." Once their supplier's plant is back on line, we may never see them again. But, on the other hand, this may be an opportunity to help the Jones Company out of a jam, to make a friend, and perhaps lay the groundwork for an ongoing relationship.

So, there's good news and bad news about abnormal demand. The good news is that it's a chance for increased sales and it's an opportunity to acquire a new and continuing customer. The downside of abnormal demand is that, unless managed properly, it can cause problems. We may miss shipments to existing customers because we're diverting resources to the abnormal order, plus the abnormal order itself may not be shipped on time or complete, due to pressure from existing customers for their orders.

Please note the words "managed properly." That's the key to this abnormal demand business: managing it effectively. Let's raise some questions:

- <u>What is abnormal demand?</u> Typically it's demand that's not in the forecast. It also tends to be large and lumpy.

- <u>How to detect it?</u> Most often, abnormal demand orders show up on a non-typical basis because they come from customers with whom we've not been doing business. More often than not, they come in by means other than the company's normal order entry processes.

  In companies where abnormal demand is likely to enter via the normal order entry channels, it's a good idea to have some kind of filter set in the order entry system, prior to Available-to-Promise time. One simple approach is merely to use a percentage of one month's forecast. In other words, if the order is for 100, and the forecast is 150, and the filter is set at 50 percent, then that order would be kicked out to a human being for a decision.

- <u>Who decides what to do?</u> Here again, we place decision-making responsibility with Sales. These people are by far the best equipped to make a decision that might help the company acquire a new customer but could negatively impact current customers. These decisions should not be left up to the folks in Operations; they're not as close to the customers.

  On the other hand, Operations has an advisory role. Sales needs to hear from Operations about its ability to meet the abnormal demand while protecting current customer commitments.

There's another set of questions to be asked. These are ones the decision-makers need to answer while making their decision:

- <u>Is this order part of the forecast?</u> Most times, the answer will be no. This means that it offers the opportunity for incremental business but may present capacity and material problems in Operations. If the abnormal demand is actually in the forecast but slated for different time periods, then dealing with it typically presents less of a resource challenge; material and capacity are or will be available, and the main issue might be one of timing. In our example above, the Jones order was not part of the forecast[3].

- <u>What is the impact on other customers?</u> This is the information owed by Operations. They might be saying that to ship Jones complete, we'd have to short the Smith order by 30 percent and we'll be a week late shipping the order for Ajax. However, if Jones can get by with less, we should be able to protect both the Smith and Ajax orders.

- <u>What does the customer really need?</u> Does Jones really need all 80 in Week 6? Or perhaps do they need 10 per week beginning in Week 6 for eight weeks? If so, this is an entirely different situation and one that should be much easier to deal with. Well, if Jones doesn't need all 80 in Week 6, why would they order that way? We don't know, but it happens frequently. Maybe they were trying to be helpful by "bothering" us with only one order versus eight. Maybe they're concerned about having to deal with eight shipments versus one, and the related freight costs. Maybe we give a price break when a customer orders 80.

Finding out what the customer really needs is a key part of managing abnormal demand.

One detail to keep in mind regarding abnormal demand: These orders need to be uniquely coded to identify them as abnormal, both while they're active and later when they're sent to the demand history file. The statistical forecasting system needs to know to ignore abnormal demand orders as it is making forecasts based on past demand patterns. If not, it will roll the abnormal demand into the forecast, when in fact abnormal demand for specific items is not repetitive. On the other hand, if the abnormal demand came from a company that subsequently became an ongoing customer, then the sales history should probably be adjusted to include that demand.

To resolve this issue and to make the right call might require a fair amount of time by the person in Sales & Marketing charged with decision-making responsibility: talking with

---

[3] If an order not in the forecast is accepted, it should not consume the forecast. On the other hand, if the order is in the forecast but in different time periods, then that forecast should be consumed.

Operations, making phone calls to the Jones company, and possibly phone calls or e-mails to current customers such as Smith and Ajax. More and more companies are setting up a position in Sales & Marketing called "Demand Manager" and assigning to it this abnormal demand responsibility plus other activities. More on this in just a moment.

Is there any way to make this abnormal demand issue a bit less challenging? Yes, we've seen companies do a good job in handling what one of them called "windfall business" (their term for abnormal demand). Company H defined this as business that is not forecasted, that does not come from regular customers, and that presents a real opportunity for increased sales. They would get a number of these orders in a typical month and, as you might suspect, they were disruptive and difficult to handle.

In their planning processes, they made formal provisions for this windfall business. They forecasted the windfall business in aggregate. They made provisions for it in their supply planning processes by reserving capacity and by hedging on certain key raw materials. Then, when the windfall business came in, they had a much better opportunity to satisfy those customers while protecting their current, ongoing customers.

What would happen if the windfall order called for a material that they hadn't hedged, or that required equipment in which they hadn't reserved capacity? Well, they were no worse off with that order than they would have been without the windfall program. They would deal with it as well as they could, and sometimes they could help the new customer and other times they couldn't.

What would happen in those weeks when no windfall business came in? They would run stock product or, alternatively, run some make-to-order business early. In effect, they used a small part of the finished goods inventory as a surge tank to enable them to deal effectively with most of the windfall business. They made a lot of friends. They converted windfall business into ongoing relationships with companies that became good customers. They captured business from their competition and drove 'em nuts.

The Demand Manager

Quite a few companies have created the function of Demand Manager. Depending on the size of the organization, this is sometimes a full-time activity, sometimes part-time, and sometimes requires more than one person. Here's a list of some of the duties that we see assigned to the demand management position:

- Assist Sales & Marketing management in sales forecasting.

- Coordinate the demand planning phase of the monthly Sales & Operations Planning cycle.

- Participate in the supply planning phase of the monthly Sales & Operations Planning cycle.

- Work closely with the Master Scheduler on demand and supply issues at the mix level.

- Coordinate decisions on product availability during periods of short supply.

- Help to resolve abnormal demand issues.

Frequently we see that the person charged with these kinds of demand management activities also has other responsibilities: serving as inside sales manager, heading up the customer service/order entry function and/or performing other sales administration duties.

However it's organized, this is an important job. Steve Souza, a principal with the Oliver Wight group, says: "Many see the Demand Manager's job as a key managerial position in the Sales/Marketing organization . . . one highly respected by both the VP of Sales & Marketing and the president. Most often, they heed his or her advice."

Gripes and Tips

Gripe: *We know the forecast is going to be wrong, so why do it?*

The ability to exercise some degree of management and control over customer demand is one of the reasons that the forecast does not have to be super-accurate. Rick Wright, Director of Sales & Operations Planning at Senco Products says: "The forecast should always be 100 percent accurate . . . if the lead time is zero." In effect, what Rick is saying is that — very close in — you're dealing with the known, with customer orders that are certain.

Here's another look at the relevant principle:

> **Principle #10: As soon as possible, replace the unknown with the known.**

CHAPTER 8

GETTING STARTED

Gripe: *We start a lot of stuff around here,*
but we don't finish much.

We've presented a new approach to forecasting that can help to get excellent results —
if implemented *properly*. The operative word here is *properly*, and we'll come back to that.

Implementing by the ABCs

In Chapter 3, we identified the ABCs of forecasting processes:

The A item is the people.
The success of a forecasting improvement initiative
will depend almost totally on the people:
their dedication, their willingness, their knowledge.

The B item is the data.
The validity and utility of the input data is of
more significance than the C item.

The C item is the computer software and hardware.
Essential, but not the critically important item.

What follows is a series of checklists organized according to the ABC principle. These
checklists are designed to direct your attention to the important aspects of each element, to
ensure that they're properly addressed. Let's start with the most important one.

The A Item: People

Among the key people to be involved in forecasting, there should be broad consensus — if not unanimity — about the following:

A1   A willingness to forecast frequently and sufficiently far into the future.

A2   Acceptance by Sales & Marketing of accountability for forecasting.

A3   A belief that better forecasts can yield better customer service, more efficient production, and lower inventories.

A4   An acceptance that the key to better forecasts is process improvement, focusing on causes of error, not forecast accuracy.

A5   Insight into why eliminating bias in the forecasts is more important than increasing forecast accuracy.

A6   An understanding that 1) less forecasting is often better, 2) that aggregate, volume forecasts should be used wherever possible, and 3) that the company should operate with only one forecast expressed in different ways.

A7   A realization that forecasts are merely a means to an end, and that the uncertainty contained within the forecasts should be replaced as soon as possible by the certainty of actual demand.

In addition, some organizational issues are important here.

A8   A willingness by key people to invest some time in improving the company's forecasting processes.

A9   The creation of a cross-functional Project Team (Design Team, Task Force, or whatever) to spearhead and manage the implementation of better forecasting processes. This team should consist of people from Sales & Marketing, Operations, Finance, and possibly New Product Development, and be headed up by a Sales & Marketing person, possibly the Demand Manager.

A10   Clear access by the Project Team to the executive group, with a mandate from them to report progress frequently.

Now if you're thinking that many of the above items seem similar to our set of forecasting principles, you're right. So how do you go about getting all or most of the key players to understand these points and buy into them?

The answer: education, which leads to understanding, which leads to a willingness to do one's job differently. For many companies, we believe that having the key players read this book will get most of the education job done. Then, subsequently, within one or several meetings, the rest of the learning can take place via discussions and the hammering out of specific tasks.

Should you bring in an outsider to teach your people and to help facilitate the related discussions? Our answer here ranges from "possibly" to "probably." If the relationship between Sales & Marketing and Operations[1] is adversarial, if some of the key people seem highly resistant to change, if the organization has a history of starting lots of initiatives and not completing many — then the outside expert will almost certainly be a good idea. Often, this is not an issue because the outsider is already present, involved with a larger project. Read on.

The Implementation Environment

Implementing better forecasting processes can happen under three different sets of conditions:

1. As a stand-alone activity.

2. As part of an implementation of Sales & Operations Planning (S&OP).

3. As part of an overall implementation of Enterprise Resource Planning (ERP), which by definition includes S&OP and/or Supply Chain Management (SCM).

In all but the first case, most companies will utilize outside resources to advise the management team on the implementation, to educate, and in general to help bring the project to a successful conclusion. Thus the outsider is already on board, and can lend a hand with the forecasting part of the larger project.

Please note the end of that last sentence: the forecasting part of the larger project. We're recommending that, when implementing S&OP, ERP, or SCM, you improve your forecasting processes as a part of that activity. It's win-win. These powerful tools will work better with better forecasts; better forecasts will have more impact when they're feeding S&OP, ERP, and/or SCM processes.

---

[1] Key people from Operations and Finance should be part of this education process.

The B Item: Data

Here are the data-related items we recommend you address:

B1   Existing external data (economic outlook, industry trends, competitor status, etc.) reviewed for validity and usefulness.

B2   Desired new external data identified and obtained.

B3   Internal data reviewed for validity and completeness, and improved where necessary and practical.

Regarding internal data, a good situation is to have three or more years of past *demand* history. Demand history means when the customers wanted the product. The problem with using shipment data as demand history is that it is "corrupted" by late shipments, partial shipments, backorders, and so forth. Basing forecasts on shipment data runs the risk of perpetuating the bad things that went on before.

So what if all you have is shipment data? Many companies don't save bookings, but almost all of them do keep sales/shipment history. If you're in that category, get started using shipment data, but do two things:

- Review the shipment history and clean it up as well as you can. Go through all the A items in the product line and as many of the Bs as possible. Manually change whatever stands out as wrong. For example, several months in a row of no shipments on a high-volume product most likely doesn't mean that there was no customer demand during that time; rather, you probably didn't ship for two months. Fix those kinds of problems. Get knowledgeable people involved in this: folks from Sales, from Customer Service/Order Entry, from Production Scheduling.

- Start right away to capture and save bookings data and use that in your statistical forecasting processes. As you start this, make sure that you truly understand the data: Does it mean what you think it means; is it complete or are there gaps in what's being collected; are the maintenance transactions — adds, changes, cancellations — being captured?

A little while ago we mentioned the desirability of having *three years* of demand history. This helps the forecasting software determine if a given item is truly seasonal.

One year of history is not enough data to make that call. Two years is better but not good. Three years or more is the best.

If you have less than two years (though we see few companies in this category), get started anyway but recognize that there may be some items that are truly seasonal but that the forecasting software can't identify as such. Here also, a manual review might be needed to specify those seasonal items as seasonal to the forecasting system.

The C Item: Software

There's bad news and good news here, and the good news far outweighs the bad. The bad news is that there are far fewer software packages for forecasting than for, say, ERP. The good news is that there are far fewer software packages for forecasting than for ERP. Because the marketplace is less crowded, the selection process is easier. In addition, the products in general are quite good and some of them are quite reasonably priced. Lee Wallace, Support Services Manager with Caelus Inc. in Spokane WA, says it well: "You don't need to spend $50,000 to $100,000 or more for software to do good forecasting. It's all about people and processes . . . not software." Appendix C, prepared by software expert Chris Gray, profiles some of the leading suppliers of forecasting software.

We believe that there are two essential attributes for forecasting software. First, it should be easy to understand. Remember Pete Skurla's caveat: If you can't explain it, don't use it. Second, it needs to have good data handling capabilities — the roll-up and blow-down processes we discussed in Chapter 5.

This leads us to the three items for software:

C1   Software to be selected (or currently being used) contains simple, transparent, easy-to-understand logic.

C2   Software to be selected (or currently being used) contains good data handling capabilities: powerful, user friendly, and expedient ways to roll-up and blow-down; to manipulate data for variance and bias analysis; and so on.

C3   Users who will be hands-on with the software are thoroughly trained in its use and can explain how it works and where the numbers come from.

Figure 8-1 recaps the steps involved in getting started.

Figure 8-1

CHECKLIST TO GET STARTED

A1   A willingness to forecast frequently and sufficiently far into the future.

A2   Acceptance by Sales & Marketing of accountability for forecasting.

A3   A belief that better forecasts can yield better customer service, more efficient production, and lower inventories.

A4   An acceptance that the key to better forecasts is process improvement, focusing on causes of error, not forecast accuracy.

A5   Insight into why eliminating bias in the forecasts is more important than increasing forecast accuracy.

A6   An understanding that 1) less forecasting often better, 2) that aggregate, volume forecasts should be used wherever possible, and 3) that the company should operate with only one forecast expressed in different ways.

A7   A realization that forecasts are merely a means to an end, and that the uncertainty contained within the forecasts should be replaced as soon as possible by the certainty of actual demand.

A8   A willingness by key people to invest some time in improving the company's forecasting processes.

A9   The creation of a cross-functional Project Team (Design Team, Task Force, or whatever) to spearhead and manage the implementation of better forecasting processes. This team should consist of people from Sales & Marketing, Operations, Finance, and possibly New Product Development, and be headed up by a Sales & Marketing person, possibly the Demand Manager.

A10 Clear access by the Project Team to the executive group, with a mandate from them to report progress frequently.

B1   Existing external data (economic outlook, industry trends, competitor status, etc.) reviewed for validity and usefulness.

B2   Desired new external data identified and obtained.

B3   Internal data reviewed for validity and completeness, and improved where necessary and practical.

C1   Software to be selected (or currently being used) contains simple, transparent, easy-to-understand logic.

C2   Software to be selected (or currently being used) that contains good data handling capabilities – powerful, user friendly, and expedient ways to roll-up and blow-down; to manipulate data for variance and bias analysis; and so on.

C3   Users who will be hands-on with the software are thoroughly trained in its use, and can explain how it works and where the numbers come from.

The Project Team

This is the pivotal group in acquiring better forecasting. It is charged with designing the new forecasting processes and managing their implementation.

Here, in very general terms, are the kinds of people that we recommend be part of this group:

- Project Leader (a relatively senior person, from Sales & Marketing)

- Product Managers

- Demand Manager

- Customer Service Manager

- Forecast Analyst

- Systems Person

- Representative from Operations (e.g., Supply Chain Manager, Materials Manager, Master Scheduler)

- Representative from Finance & Accounting (e.g., Controller, Accounting Manager)

- Others as appropriate, possibly a person from New Product Development.

Early on, the Project Team develops the mission/vision statement for the project, spelling out what the organization is trying to accomplish and how things will look after they get there. We recommend that most or all of the following goals be included in that statement:

We will forecast less, not more.

We will focus on process improvement, not forecast accuracy.

We will emphasize teamwork and open communications.

*We will encourage Operations to increase flexibility
in Manufacturing and Purchasing.*

The mission/vision statement should be approved by the executive group.

The Project Team draws up the written project plan and then manages activities to make it happen. This plan should include the checklists contained in this chapter and should also reflect timing, pilot and cutover schedules, and the like. We recommend that the Project Team meet once per week, for about an hour, and report progress to the executive staff every other week. It should address the items called out above, plus others as required.

A well managed project should start to return significant benefits within three months. A smaller organization may have the project completed within that time and the Project Team can begin to meet less frequently. After six months the new processes should be well embedded in the operating climate of the company, at which time the Project Team can disband.

 A full implementation in a larger company may take considerably longer — possibly up to a year; however, substantial benefits should be realized in increments along the way. In this case, as with any long-term project, we recommend that the project be scheduled very tightly, with deliverables called for every 30 to 90 days.

Gripes and Tips

Gripe: *We start a lot of stuff around here, but we don't finish much.*

Tip: Do it as spelled out in this chapter and your odds for getting far better forecasting processes — quickly — will be very high.

CHAPTER 9

WRAP UP

Gripe: *In Operations, we're victims of Marketing's lousy forecasts. And there's nothing we can do.*

Companies can make great strides in their ability to service customers by improving their forecasting. They can improve their forecasting by following the three fundamentals that form the basis of this book.

1. Forecast Less, Not More

Independent Versus Dependent Demand Revisited

Over 40 years ago, a very intelligent, hardworking guy named Joe Orlicky, working in a planning and scheduling capacity at the J. I. Case Company in Racine WI, spelled out the differences between independent and dependent demand. Joe said that independent demand is that which comes in to the company from the outside, from customers. As such, it needs to be forecasted. L.L. Bean has to forecast how many hiking boots it's going to sell.

Dependent demand, on the other hand, can be for components required to support a production schedule within the plant. The company making boots for L.L. Bean needs to know how much leather it will need, but it should not forecast that future demand. That demand is *dependent* on the production plan for boots. Dependent demand, Joe Orlicky told us, should be *calculated* from the "upstream" production schedule. This approach typically results in a much more valid estimate of future demand, even recognizing that those upstream schedules can change.

Isn't this obvious? Yes. But for those of us laboring in this field back then, it was a revelation. This concept — independent versus dependent demand — is a bedrock principle that underlies much of the Resource Planning body of knowledge. So, here's a tip of the hat to Joe Orlicky.

But . . . we need to mentally extend this principle a bit farther. Companies whose products are primarily used in other manufacturers' products are dealing with dependent rather than independent demand. The opportunity is to get out of forecasting mode and into a collaborative planning process with those manufacturers.

This of course is happening today much more than it was just ten years ago, and we'll see more of it in the future because:

- It yields better results.

- Thanks to technology, it's getting easier to communicate effectively across company boundaries.

- More manufacturing companies will get their Resource Planning processes working properly as they get their inventory records and bills of material cleaned up and stabilize their Master Schedules.

Bottom line: Very little demand is truly independent. Think *dependent*. Be on the lookout for how you can get a direct handle on your customers dependent demand — particularly inside the Planning Time Fence — thereby reducing the amount of forecasting you need to do and simultaneously getting better numbers on which to base future plans.

Avoid the Suicide Quadrant

In the following figures, the area in the upper right is what we call the "Suicide Quadrant." We call it that because that's where you can drive yourself nuts; it's where you would be forecasting in lots of detail far out into the future. Throughout this book, we've been trying to help you stay out of the Suicide Quadrant because it usually doesn't yield good results. There are better ways to get the information you need; forecasting within the Suicide Quadrant is a lot of work and you're too busy to do busy work.

A few words of explanation about the following diagrams: First, the horizontal axis represents time, with the near term to the left and the far term to the right. Forecasts are less certain in the far term. Second, the vertical axis represents the detail to be forecasted, with aggregated families of products at the low end, and end items toward the top. Forecasts with greater amounts of detail, i.e., end items, are apt to have much more forecast error.

Figure 9-1 represents a forecasting process far into the future at the end item level of detail. Keep in mind:

- Doing a better job of forecasting in this quadrant will not result in much improvement.

- Staying in this quadrant, in today's business climate, is not a sustainable proposition for the long run.

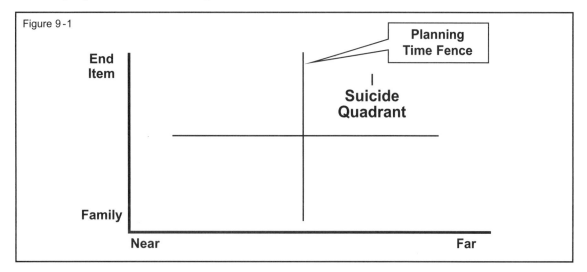

Figure 9-2 illustrates getting out of the Suicide Quadrant and moving into Quadrant II, the Aggregate Only Quadrant.

- Rough-cut planning is used to anticipate required resources in both capacity and materials.

- Detail is needed only when moving inside the Planning Time Fence.

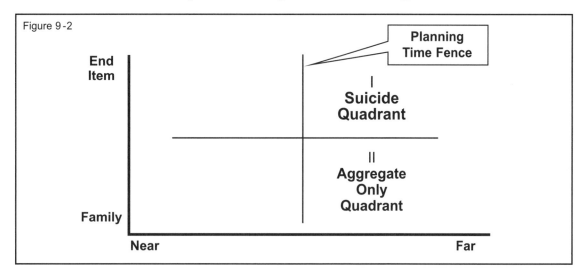

The next figure, 9-3, shows the Customer Schedule Quadrant. Here, information directly from the customer is used for most or all of the detail needed inside the Planning Time Fence. Three ways to arrive at the detail for this quadrant are:

1. Detailed mix forecasts (by end item), or

2. Customer orders or schedules, or

3. A combination of both.

With the e-commerce tools available, it will become easier for companies to collaborate with their customers, and get schedules electronically. The challenge will continue to be to ensure that those schedules are valid and that they represent what the customer truly needs.

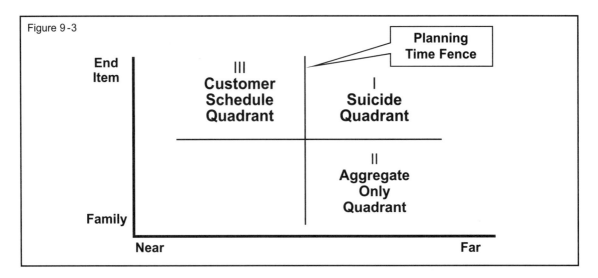

Figure 9-3

The Agility Quadrant, shown in Figure 9-4, represents the ultimate goal: flexible supplier and production resources that can handle any mix of product within the volume forecast, quickly.

It essentially represents a shortening of the area inside the Planning Time Fence to a point where a company can build any product after it gets the customer order or schedule. While most companies may never achieve this objective for *all* of their products, it should still be the direction in which a company strives to move. In summary: Stay out of the Suicide Quadrant (#1). Forecast at the aggregate, volume level into the future (Quadrant #2), quite possibly using planning bills; this will result in a sharp drop in the amount of forecasting you'll need to do. Through close collaboration with customers, obtain their schedules and translate them into schedules for yourselves (Quadrant #3); this could further reduce the need to forecast. Finally, reduce lead times so much that you'll be able to buy and produce so quickly that the need to do detailed forecasting goes away (Quadrant #4).

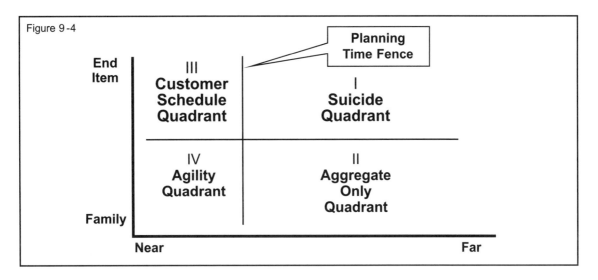

Figure 9-4

Planning Bills — An Interim Step?

Planning bills of material (covered in Chapter 5) can be a big help in getting out of the Suicide Quadrant (#1) and into Quadrant #2. They allow an aggregate forecast to be easily broken down into projected demand for components. Having these components in stock enables a company to finish to order, avoiding detailed forecasting at the end item level. This is a major improvement because far fewer items will be forecasted.

However, as we just saw, this may be only an interim step. After all, the percentages used in planning bills are themselves a type of forecast and, as such, they will have to be maintained, they will be wrong, they frequently require safety stock (hedges), and so on.

The best solution of all: Cut lead times for not only the finishing operations, but also for components and materials. This *theoretically* would give you the ability to make totally to order; you could make the product so quickly that the need for planning bills might eventually go away.

Will companies ever get there? Yes, some are there today — mostly companies with relatively simpler products. Some companies, perhaps those with highly complex products, may never get there. But many companies, perhaps those "in the middle" of the product complexity scale, can and should move in that direction.

2. Emphasize Teamwork, Not Formulas

Things like customer connectivity and collaborative forecasting can be major helps in enabling a company to ship on time all the time and not have ten tons of inventory laying around. Our colleague at Ohio State, Bill Berry, points out that the idea is to substitute information for inventory. It's not necessary to "brute force" good customer service via mountains of inventory; rather, good service can be "finessed" by means of having valid information regarding customers' future plans and intentions and basing future actions upon that. This means working together, cooperating, and sharing information.

It's time for another forecasting principle: **There is far more to be gained by people collaborating and communicating well than by all of the advanced formulas and algorithms yet developed.**

Teamwork and the Internet

Neither of your authors is an expert on the Internet, and so we turned to two people who know a lot more about it than we do. John M. Paterson, a senior executive within IBM's purchasing operations, had this to say:

> "The real value of Web services is in the integration of the supply chain rather than in being able to plug suppliers in and out based on price. Web-based services that tout spot buying and options are of little value to large manufacturers. (Authors' comment: and probably not of great value for medium and small manufacturers either.) We want to develop continuity, quality, assured levels of supply from our OEMs. You don't develop lasting relationships with large suppliers from spot markets and option buys . . . .

> "Our Web tools have enabled us to have a much more open relationship with our suppliers. Today, they have direct access to data on IBM. . . . This is vital to creating the tightly coupled relationships on which we depend."[1]

Our colleague, Chris Gray of Gray Research in New Hampshire, also shared his views on how the Internet will play into forecasting and collaborative planning:

> "I acknowledge that the Internet is a powerful tool to help people communicate and share information. However, so far there have been only limited applications and opportunities for sharing forecasts and demand data among trading partners.

---

[1] Latamore, Bert. "Get Personal: An Interview with IBM's John M. Paterson," *APICS — The Performance Advantage*, October 2000 Issue, Volume 10 No. 10.

"I expect to see future Web services that emphasize collaborative forecasting techniques among multiple trading partners across the value chain. I expect to see situations where there is enough visibility across the chain that the multiple, sometimes redundant planning organizations at each trading partner are consolidated: one planning organization to ensure product availability for multiple supply chain nodes.

"Further, I expect Internet-based replenishment approaches that will leverage the kinds of kanban capabilities that have made Lean Manufacturing such an important approach. E-kanban signals have the potential to synchronize the supply chain just as visual signals have synchronized our factories. We see the power of the Internet being used to drive down supply chain costs and increase flexibility — the kinds of things that can give *all* the trading partners a competitive advantage!"

3. Focus on Process Improvement, Not Forecast Accuracy

Here we're talking not about forecasting processes, but rather the processes used in Operations — Manufacturing, Purchasing, Distribution, etc. — to buy materials, make the product, and get it to the customers. These processes also can play a major role in making forecasts better.

One of the forecaster's best friends goes by the handle "Lean Manufacturing" or its predecessor "Just-in-Time." These are outside of the traditional world of forecasting and are primarily seen on the Operations side of the business. These tools place great emphasis on increasing plant and supplier flexibility, shortening lead times, and reducing complexity. One example is the approach known as "kanban," described in Appendix E.

Another is cellular manufacturing, where intermittent production is replaced by flow. Yet another is quick changeover, and we'd like to get into the details of that for just a bit, primarily for those readers from the demand side of the business who may not be familiar with its benefits.

Quick Changeover

Many companies have achieved 50 to 75 percent or greater decreases in set-up time with amazingly low investment, and they've done it quickly. These "smart" companies then use some of the money they've freed up out of the inventories to fund further set-up reductions, driving their changeover times down even more. As a result, they've been able to sharply reduce their run sizes with no increase in changeover cost and no decrease in output. Think about it this way: Reducing changeover time by 75 percent makes it practical to cut run sizes from, say, one month's supply down to one week's supply. The benefits:

- Shorter runs mean fewer stockouts. This is because the company can cycle through the product line much faster. They're not "as far away" in the cycle from running a product that might be headed for a stockout.

- Shorter runs can mean shorter lead times, for the same reason.

- Shorter runs mean lower inventories. By putting one week's supply into inventory at a time, rather than one month's worth, the lot size component of the inventory should drop sharply. Safety stock should go down also, because less forward protection is needed.

It doesn't get much better than this. Reducing changeovers gives a company the ability to do a far better job of servicing customers through better customer service and shorter lead times, and it typically can do this with higher plant efficiencies and far lower inventories. And, of course, as lead times shorten, the Planning Time Fence moves in closer and thus the need to do detailed, mix forecasting lessens and may even go away completely[2].

Location, Location, Location

As well as being the three most important things in real estate, location can be an important part of operational flexibility. *Where* the product is finished can make a big difference.

One of the key elements of flexibility is to add the optionality into the product after the customers tell you what they want, and do it quickly — which of course is one of the bases for the planning bill approach we discussed earlier.

Well, if you ship your products from distribution centers (DCs) rather than from the plant, what does that say about where the product should be finished? If you finish the product at the plant for shipment to the DCs, then it's a make-to-stock situation, and you'll have to lock in the options before you're sure of exactly what the customers want. *You will need to forecast at the detailed, mix level.* Avoid that if you possibly can, because that's the road to higher inventories, lower customer service, and increased frustration.

---

[2] For more on this extremely important topic, we recommend the SMED book, written by Shigeo Shingo, one of the most brilliant industrial engineers who ever lived: *A Revolution in Manufacturing: The SMED System.* Portland, OR: Productivity Press, 1985.

Let's start thinking outside the box. Must all of the value-adding activities be done at the plant? If you finish the product in the DCs, then you may be able to complete the product *after* you receive the customer order. In effect, the product becomes finish-to-order.

Where it's practical, make the components, parts, modules, base product, and so forth at the plant and ship them in a semi-finished state to the DCs. Let the DCs finish the product after the customers tell them exactly what they want. Defer adding the optionality not only until the latest possible point in time, but also to the best possible point on the map. That's normally the location that's closest to the customer.

The above topics — quick changeover and location — are but two of a number of topics that bear on this entire issue of plant and supplier flexibility. For more on these very important issues, you might want to check several books called out in the Bibliography: *Agile Competitors and Virtual Organizations* by Steven Goldman et al. and *Just-in-Time: Making It Happen* by Bill Sandras.

Let's revisit the gripe we saw at the start of this chapter: *In Operations, we're victims of Marketing's lousy forecasts. And there's nothing we can do.* As you might have guessed by now, we don't buy that. Here's how we see it, as expressed in our twelfth and final forecasting principle: **Better processes yield better results; better production, purchasing, and scheduling processes help yield better forecasts.**

Principles of Forecasting

It might be helpful to take a look at all of our principles in one place, just to get the big picture. They're shown in Figure 9-5.

Boiling down these principles might go like this: All companies must forecast. Sales & Marketing owns the forecast, and the forecast must make sense in the overall scheme of things. Forecast mix only where you have to. Focus on better processes, on reducing forecast error, and on eliminating bias. Run the business with only one set of forecast numbers, and don't rely on the forecast any longer than you have to. Nurture teamwork within the company and also with your customers. The Operations group can play a major role in getting better forecasts by improving processes in their part of the business to increase speed and agility.

Figure 9-5

PRINCIPLES OF FORECASTING

Principle #1:   Sales forecasting is being done in virtually every company that produces and sells products, either formally or by default. The challenge is to do it well, better than the competition.

Principle #2:   Better forecasts enable companies to give higher customer service (order fill) to lower the inventories, to run the plants better, to work more cooperatively with suppliers, and — last but certainly not least — to sell more product.

Principle #3:   Sales & Marketing people own the sales forecast; they are accountable for its development, authorization, and execution.

Principle #4:   The forecast can and must make sense based on the big picture: economic outlook, industry trends, market share, and so on.

Principle #5:   Better processes yield better results; better forecasting processes yield better forecasts.

Principle #6:   The best way to increase forecast accuracy is to focus on reducing forecast error.

Principle #7:   Bias is the worst kind of forecast error; strive for zero bias.

Principle #8:   Forecast the volume; manage the mix. Wherever possible, forecast at higher, aggregate levels. Forecast in detail only where necessary.

Principle #9.   One forecast, many views. Have only one forecast, with the ability to display it in a variety of ways for different uses.

Principle #10:   As soon as possible, replace the unknown with the known.

Principle #11:   There is far more to be gained by people collaborating and communicating well than by all of the advanced formulas and algorithms yet developed.

Principle #12:   Better processes yield better results; better production, purchasing, and scheduling processes help yield better forecasts.

Into the Future

Now it's time for your fearless authors to peer confidently into the future and try to determine what it'll look like. (Please keep in mind that there are no warranties on these predictions.) Here goes:

- As more manufacturers and their suppliers adopt Lean Manufacturing, less mix forecasting will be necessary. Companies will be more aware of the Suicide Quadrant and the need to get out of there and stay out.

- Collaborative planning and forecasting techniques will be more widely used.

- Companies supplying OEMs (original equipment manufacturers) will benefit greatly as many of these OEMs finally learn how to use Resource Planning processes properly, with accurate data and a stable master schedule. Many OEMs today have the ability to transfer schedules electronically; the problem is that those schedules aren't valid.

- Planning bills of material will still be used, but a growing number of companies will find them no longer necessary due to high plant and supplier flexibility and the resulting ultra-short lead times.

- Twenty years from now, forecasting will be easier and forecasts will be better than they are today. Forecasting will be less contentious and there'll be less finger pointing. The hassles won't be completely gone, but they'll be lessened.

- To say it another way, more and more companies will make the journey out of the Suicide Quadrant into the Aggregate Only Quadrant, the Customer Schedule Quadrant, and ultimately, the Agility Quadrant.

We hope, and we believe, that these things will come about. Of course, some leading- edge companies are already there. Perhaps your company should join them in a world where forecasting is easier and forecasts are better.

APPENDIXES

Appendix A

PLANNING TIME FENCE

In this book, we're using Planning Time Fence to mean the time frame inside of which detailed planning must be present in the Master Schedule. The factors that determine its length are as follows:

- The cumulative manufacturing and purchasing lead time for the product.

- Manufacturing lead time only, if planning bills of material are being used.

- If a product is cycled (campaigned) in manufacturing (for example: run only once every three months), then the Planning Time Fence would be three months.

The Master Schedule inside the Planning Time Fence must be under the control of the Master Scheduler. This is necessary to provide the desired level of detail and to avoid changes that will adversely affect customer deliveries, capacities, costs, and inventories.

It can be specified for an individual item or a group of items. For example, a product made in the U.S. plant may have a cumulative lead time of three weeks while the lead time for a very similar product outsourced from the Orient might be six months. The Planning Time Fence for these two items would be about three weeks for the former and six months for the latter.

A secondary meaning of Planning Time Fence is software oriented: It is that point inside of which the Master Scheduling software is not allowed to plan or modify replenishment orders. This feature is important in order to keep control — and hence accountability — with the Master Scheduler.

Appendix B

FORECASTING METHODOLOGIES

Throughout this book, we've emphasized the importance of teamwork, not formulas; forecast less, not more; focus on process improvement, not accuracy. However, in most companies, there is a need to use mathematical models as part of the forecasting process. The objective of this appendix is not to fully explain each alternative, but to summarize some of the more popular alternatives.

There are generally five categories of forecasting methodologies. They are listed below with some examples of each:

Basic Techniques

These approaches use demand history to identify existing behavior based on four patterns: level (horizontal), trend (increase or decrease), seasonality (repetitive highs and lows), and noise (random fluctuation). Examples are:

- Simple Average — the forecast for future periods is the average of all sales that have occurred in the past. This technique will dampen fluctuations.

- Moving Average — the forecast for future periods is the average of only a specified number of recent months. The number of months is a user determined variable.

- Exponential Smoothing — this technique places a heavier weight on the more recent periods and lesser weights on older periods at a decreasing exponential rate. The weighted factor (called alpha) is user determined. (See Appendix H.)

- Adaptive Smoothing — a variation of exponential smoothing that automatically selects the weighted factor (alpha) based on the previous period's error.

Focus Forecasting

This technique steps back in time and compares actual sales to a forecast generated by a number of models (about 20) to determine which, if used, would have produced the least error. It then gives the user the opportunity to accept this as the model for the future forecast.

Advanced Techniques

These techniques also use demand history in the same way as the fundamental techniques, but they use unique formulas to project the future. Examples of this category are: Box Jenkins, Autoregressive Moving Average, Decomposition Analysis, Spectral Analysis, and Fourier Analysis.

Regression (Correlation) Analysis

This technique also uses demand history, but in a way that establishes a relationship with data other than sales history, such as: price increases, advertising, the economy, product quality, housing starts, the price of gold, birth rate, etc. This relationship is then used to mathematically predict the future.

Qualitative Techniques

These subjective techniques turn the opinions of experienced experts into formulas from which a forecast is then generated. Many of these techniques represent very broad and general definitions. Some are: Delphi, Market Research, Panel Consensus, and Sales Force Composite.

The bibliography also lists related sources of information.

Appendix C

PARTIAL LISTING OF SUPPLIERS OF FORECASTING SOFTWARE

Compiled by:
Chris Gray, Gray Research
cgray@grayresearch.com
603-522-5310

Below is a list of software suppliers who specialize in business forecasting software, along with some selected information on the functions of the software. Most of the information was taken from publicly available sources including the respective company Web sites. In many cases, additional information is available at those same Web sites.

Automatic Forecasting Systems, Inc.	Infor Global Solutions
B. T. Smith & Associates	Logility
Business Forecast Systems, Inc.	Manugistics Group, Inc.
Demand Management, Inc.	McConnell Chase Software Works
Demand Works	Prescient Systems
Demantra	SAS
E/Step Software Inc.	Smart Software
Futurion	Supply Chain Consultants
John Galt Solutions, Inc.	

AUTOMATIC FORECASTING SYSTEMS
P O Box 563
Hatboro PA 19040

Software Name: Autobox
Phone: 215 675-0652
www.autobox.com

Commentary: Autobox is an objective, statistical, extrapolative forecasting system that uses a rule-based heuristics system approach to ARIMA (univariate) and Transfer Function (causal) modeling.

The system provides an automated approach to modeling of time series using both the history of that time series and the history of possible user-suggested causal variables. This model is often called a Polynomial Distributed Lag or a Dynamic Regression or more collectively the class of Box-Jenkins Models. It augments this class by enhancing the model with empirically identified Intervention Variables such as Local Time Trends, Level Shifts, Seasonal Pulses and One-time Pulses yielding a robust model. These tools can produce forecasts for large numbers of series with limited or no manual intervention. Users can pre-suggest models and/or parameters to possibly enhance model formulation. To produce more accurate forecasts, AUTOBOX automatically tailors the model to the problem at hand including selecting the best lead and lag structures for each input series and the best weightings. It corrects for omitted variables (e.g., holidays or price changes that have affected the historical data, but that the system has no knowledge of) by identifying pulses, seasonal pulses, level shifts and local time trends, and then adding the needed structure through surrogate variables. Conversely, it also eliminates unneeded structure (e.g., a statistically unimportant causal variable) to keep the model manageable. It performs all these functions as part of its normal routine without human intervention. It also reports the statistical tests used to determine the model parameters, and let users manipulate the coefficients and model structure if they want.

The modeling logic of Autobox incorporates causal factors into the forecast. These include factors such as:
- Sales of related products (e.g., shampoo and conditioner) • Cannibalization effects
- Price of competitors products

Features:
- Automatic Modeling
- Tournament Modeling
- Forecast Analysis and Diagnostics
- Complete Set of Box-Jenkins Modeling Tools
- Graphical Analysis Tools
- Database and Model Storage
- Intervention Detection of level shifts, season pulses, single point outliers and changes in the variance of the series
- Measures to Assess Forecast Model Performance

B. T. SMITH & ASSOCIATES
P. O. Box 1653
Butler PA 16003

Software Name: Focus Forecasting
Phone 724/586-2200
www.focusforecasting.com

Commentary: Focus Forecasting is a simple, non-statistical system that uses objective data and "simulation" logic to determine which of the system's simple forecasting strategies would have worked best in the recent past. For example, the system might have strategies like:
- We'll sell what we sold last year.
- We'll sell 10% more than last year.
- We'll sell what we sold the last quarter.
- We'll probably sell half as much as we sold in the last six months.

Every time Focus Forecasting® is asked to produce a forecast on an item, it tries all the strategies on the past sales for the item and calculates which one of the strategies would have worked best in the recent past for forecasting the item. This is the strategy that the system chooses for producing a forecast for future sales.

Focus Forecasting® has approximately twenty (20) forecasting strategies, similar to the ones listed above. Generally speaking, Focus Forecasting is:
- Simple: although it is based on data, there is no complicated mathematics. Forecasting strategies tend to parallel the strategies that people in sales or marketing might use in forecasting an item.

- Transparent: the forecasting process is easy to understand, and perhaps more importantly, it is possible to explain where the forecast number came from.
- Based on the idea that the most accurate predictor of the future is the recent past.

Additional functions of the software include a) import from and export to a variety of formats including MS Excel, Lotus 1-2-3, ASCII, etc., b) forecast adjustment and overrides either by specifying the forecasting strategy or entering period overrides directly, and c) forecast evaluation and best-fit selection (automatic) or specify manually.

BUSINESS FORECAST SYSTEMS, INC.
68 Leonard Street
Belmont, MA 02478

Software Name: Forecast Pro
Phone: 617 484-5050
www.forecastpro.com

Commentary: Forecast Pro is an objective, statistical, extrapolative forecasting system that uses multiple methods and a best-fit selection process. The expert system chooses among the following five classes of forecasting models:
- Simple Methods - moving average models.
- Curve Fitting - supports four types of curves - straight line, quadratic, exponential and growth.
- Low Volume Models - Croston's Intermittent Demand model and discrete data models are provided to accommodate low volume and "sparse" data (i.e., data where the demand is often zero).
- Exponential Smoothing - Twelve different Holt-Winters exponential smoothing models are provided.
- Box-Jenkins - supports a multiplicative seasonal Box-Jenkins model.

Also available in an advanced version of the software are:
- Dynamic Regression – Build causal models (generalized Cochrane-Orcutt models) that include independent variables, lagged or transformed variables.
- Event Models - Extend exponential smoothing by providing adjustments for events like promotions, strikes or other irregular occurrences, or the effects of holidays like Easter and Rosh Hashanah.
- Multiple Level Exponential Smoothing - Aggregate data into groups that can be reconciled using a top-down or bottom-up approach to produce consistent forecasts at all levels. Seasonal and event indexes can be extracted from higher level aggregates and applied to lower level data.
- Census X-11 - Factors a time series into its major constituents (trend-cycle, seasonal, trading day and irregular).

Additional functions of the software include
- Import from and export to a variety of formats including MS Excel, Lotus 1-2-3, ASCII and ODBC.
- Forecast adjustment using either a graph or spreadsheet display,
- Provides functions for documenting assumptions, overrides and adjustments.
- Expert selection (automatic) or specify manually.
- Hierarchical drill down capabilities, adjusting the forecast at one level of a hierarchy adjusts all other (appropriate) levels.

According to the company, Forecast Pro recently outperformed all other software approaches and 18 out of 19 academic teams in the Makridakis-3 study, the largest and most comprehensive empirical forecasting study ever performed.

DEMAND MANAGEMENT, INC.
150 N. Meramec, Suite 400
St. Louis, MO 63105

Software Name: Demand Solutions
Phone: 314/727-4448
www.demandsolutions.com

Commentary: Demand Solutions is a simple, non-statistical system that uses objective data and "simulation" logic to select the formula which best addresses each item's demand pattern. Like some other forecasting systems, Demand Solutions uses some simple forecasting strategies:
• We'll sell what we sold last quarter.
• We'll sell what we sold in the same quarter last year.
• We'll sell 10% less than what we sold last year.
• We'll sell 10% more than what we sold last year.

Demand Solutions includes several modules:
• DS FM (Demand Solutions Forecast Management) is the forecasting engine and data warehouse.
• DS FB (Demand Solutions Feedback) is the collaboration mechanism of the system.
• DS View (Demand Solutions Reporting and Analysis) a custom reporting and data analysis tool.
Every time Demand Solutions is asked to produce a forecast on an item, it tries all the strategies on the past sales for the item and calculates which one of the strategies would have worked best in the recent past for forecasting the item. This is the strategy that the system chooses for producing a forecast for future sales.

Demand Solutions has approximately twenty (23) forecasting strategies, similar to the ones listed above but also including some simple exponential smoothing techniques.

• The system also includes tools for:
• Making adjustments and overrides.
• Analyzing data by aggregation, rotation, filtering, sorting and other manipulations.
• Adding notes to track assumptions.
• Aggregating forecasts to family levels.

DEMAND WORKS
16 W. Market Street
West Chester PA 19382

SoftwareName: Demand Works DP
Phone: 610 701-9873
www.demandworks.com

Commentary: Demand Works DP is an objective, statistical, extrapolative forecasting system that uses multiple methods and a best-fit selection process. The forecasting engine is Forecast Pro and is licensed from Business Forecast Systems, Inc. The system supports level, trend, seasonality, events and other causal modeling, and utilizes a variety of techniques including:
• Exponential Smoothing - Single, double, or triple parameter, with support for additive or multiplicative seasonality.
• Box-Jenkins - An ARIMA approach which includes support for seasonality.
• Croston's Intermittent - A model which is particularly useful for intermittent or sporadic demand patterns.
• Moving Averages - A simple, yet popular time-series model.

- Discrete - A model based on the binomial distribution which is useful for demand that occurs in small integers.
- Multiple Regression - A technique based on correlating and/or lagging causal time-series with respect to demand. This technique is often used in aggregate or econometric forecasting.
- Event Modeling - Multiple event forecasting approaches are supported, including a smoothing-based approach, multiple regression, and a multiple-bucket curve application technique.

The expert model and parameter selection utilizes a combination of proprietary heuristics and simplex optimization techniques to select the best fitting, most predictive forecasting model. Demand Works also supports other techniques such as multi-level, multi-pyramid forecasting, as well as multiple-bucket synchronization.

Pyramid forecasting enables users to focus on aggregate levels, and allows for the inheritance of patterns from less noisy aggregate forecasts for use in detailed SKU-level planning. Demand Works DP's aggregation logic is flexible, allowing for independent synchronization of levels and pyramids, and providing for a number of proration reconciliation techniques.

DEMANTRA

767c Concord Avenue
Cambridge, Massachusetts 02138

Software Name: Demantra
Phone: 617 876-2500
www.demantra.com

Commentary: Demantra ("Demand is our Mantra") provides an objective, statistical, extrapolative forecasting system. According to the company, the forecasting techniques of the system are based on sophisticated combinative statistical analysis methods. These include exponential smoothing and ARIMA. Again according to the company "Demand Planner is the most powerful and accurate demand planning and forecasting engine of its kind."

The suite of Demantra software includes:
- Demand Planner™ - the forecasting engine.
- Demand Collaborator™ - collaborative support for multiple trading partners.
- Demand Analyzer™ - business intelligence analyzer.

Features of the system include:
- Consolidates multiple views of demand.
- Information easily accessible, actionable.
- Causal event planning included.
- Displays trends and market conditions in a variety of quickly understood reports.
- Drill downs allow access to appropriate levels of detail.
- Supports exception-driven work environment.
- Graphical, intuitive workbench interface.
- Advanced OLAP (On-line Analytical Processing) analysis of demand and product changes.
- Multi-dimensional Planning methodology includes product hierarchy, distribution network, marketing channels, etc.

- Simulations based on modifications to historical or future data.
- Advanced utilities to facilitate new product and new market planning.
- Event / promotion planning supported.

E/STEP SOFTWARE INC.

12015 Summitview Road
Yakima, WA 98908

Software Name: Finished Goods Series Demand Planner

Phone: 509 853-5000
www.estepsoftware.com

Commentary: The Finished Goods Series Demand Planner is an objective, statistical, extrapolative forecasting system that uses multiple methods including Fourier Seasonal Profiles, Winter's Base Index, moving average, exponential smoothing.

FGS uses the demand history for each SKU to compute a mathematical model of the demand, which it then projects into the future. FGS contains multiple families of forecasting models, including the Fourier Seasonal Profiles. The system's automatic model-fitting logic determines the level, trend, and appropriate seasonal cycles, if significant. The user can override these decisions.

FGS includes the ability to identify and use the forecasting calendar most appropriate to each SKU, allowing items to be forecasted bimonthly, quarterly, semiannually, or annually; even though the items reside in the same database. The forecasting calendar implementation in FGS also eliminates the error inherent in assuming that a period has the same length from one year to the next. For example, with calendar months, January could have as few as 18 or as many as 22 selling days, in different years.

FGS includes many Statistical Process Control (SPC) tools to monitor the forecasting process, identifying those SKUs which are going outside control limits, and those which are doing fine on "autopilot." FGS supports a multi-tiered forecasting approach at any user-defined levels. Summarizing and forcing forecasts (up or down) according to a pyramidal organization, can be set or changed at any time, and the system allows multiple (potentially overlapping) pyramids.

Forecasting techniques in the system include:
- Fourier Seasonal Profiles (Seasonal).
- Base Index (Seasonal Index, Winter's)
- Level
- Heuristic Modifications of the above techniques.
- Moving Average
- Exponential Smoothing
- Level and Trend

Exception conditions detected by the system are:
- Outliers
- Pattern Change
- Lumpy Demand
- All Time Supply
- High Error
- Short History
- Recommended Calendar Change - to a less frequent calendar

FUTURION

333 Sylvan Avenue, Suite 301
Englewood Cliffs, New Jersey 07632

Software Name: Futurcast

Phone: 201 541-3888
www.futurcast.com

Commentary: Futurcast is an objective, statistical, extrapolative forecasting system that uses multiple methods and an expert system selection process.

Key features of the software include:
- Expert system forecasting, exception reporting and in-depth forecast accuracy analysis.
- Filtering, automatic adjustments and pyramidal prorating functions.
- Customized territory sales/customer forecast response sheet.
- "What-if" sales forecast analysis and review module.
- Integrates marketing and field sales intelligence into the expert "baseline" forecast.
- Multi-level aggregating and goal setting.
- Budget, sales tracking and gap analysis.
- Long term and strategic forecasting.
- Executive sales analysis and reporting
- Provide mechanisms for documenting assumptions.

INFOR GLOBAL SOLUTIONS
11720 Amber Park Drive, Suite 400
Alpharetta, GA 30004

Software Name: Mercia
Phone: 866-244-5479
www.infor.com

Commentary: Mercia is an objective, statistical, extrapolative forecasting system that uses multiple methods and an Bayesian algorithm to construct the correct forecasting model for each entity. The Bayesian Dynamic Linear Modelling techniques of the software provide dynamic low-intervention statistical routines that automatically detect and adjust the best statistical model for each product.

Facilities exist to support subjective input to the forecast where future demand is not dependant solely on historical patterns. Intelligence can be drawn from a variety of sources, both internally and by collaborating externally with customers and suppliers. The end result is a stable "one number" demand plan that can be used to drive the entire supply chain.

The resulting plan is monitored on a continual basis to help manage exceptional events in the supply chain and ensure that the forecast is in line with actual demand and the budget. By focusing on what is important (exceptions and critical products) the forecasting process can be run very efficiently, with the absolute minimum manual intervention. Key features include:
- Multiple historical data streams (invoiced sales, demand, orders, point-of-sale etc.)
- Automatic calendar interpolation when developing the statistical model
- Automatic consideration of demand profile for each product type ("fast, slow moving" etc.) when selecting best forecast model
- Automatic detection of seasonality, level and trend
- Identification and auto-filter of exceptional demand
- Causal modeling to include factors like price, population, etc.
- New product launches, repackaging, new formulations and engineering changes
- Promotions, pricing, advertising and general marketing activity
- Product life cycle stages, obsolescence, predecessor-successor links
- Hierarchical planning - top down or bottom up
- Forecast adjustments done directly to statistical (tabular) data or by drag and drop against the graphical display of the forecast.

JOHN GALT SOLUTIONS, INC.
39 South LaSalle Street, Suite 815
Chicago, IL 60607

Software Name: Forecast X
Phone: 312 701-9026
www.johngalt.com

Commentary: ForecastX is an objective, statistical, extrapolative forecasting system that uses multiple methods and a best-fit selection process. The statistical forecasting techniques include including Time-Series forecasting, New Product forecasting, ARIMA Modeling and Event Modeling.

The system includes multiple modules:
- ForecastX Engine – provides the technology to support CPFR integration as well as DRP, feeds widely available Business Intelligence tools.
- ForecastX Collaborator - allows development of a collaborative planning process.
- ForecastX SDK (software development kit) – provides ActiveX controls, cross platform libraries, and Java applets to allow the forecasting functions to be embedded in external applications.
- ForecastX Wizard – provides integration with Microsoft Excel for data analysis and increased analytical power. Provides five different graphical reports to display forecasted results. Wizard identifies past trends and selects the best forecasting model. Reporting features include trend adjustment, auto-filter, and the ability to track changes and adjustments within reports.
- ForecastX BI Add-in – a plug-in provides a way to add statistical forecasting to existing Business Intelligence Tools.

Features include:
- Custom allocation and summarization based on client defined business model
- Full complement of data analysis tools including event modeling and promotional planning
- Management by exception for highlighting forecasts outside some specified range
- Customizable reports and sophisticated data analysis
- Forecasts can be reconciled at any level of business hierarchy
- Complete Allocation and Multiple Grouping Capabilities
- Database OLAP Capability

Of particular interest to anyone who would like to understand various statistical forecasting techniques: ForecastX is available on CD with the book "Business Forecasting, Fourth Edition" by J. Holt Wilson, Central Michigan University, Barry Keating, University of Notre Dame, and John Galt Solutions.

LOGILITY
470 East Paces Ferry Road
Atlanta GA 30305-3300

Software Name: Demand Chain Planning
Phone: 800/762-5207
www.logility.com

Commentary: The Demand Chain Planning modules of Logility Voyager Solutions includes an objective, statistical, extrapolative forecasting system.

The Demand Chain Planning modules of Logility are:
- Life Cycle Planning
- Demand Planning
- Demand Chain Voyager
- Event Planning
- Inventory Planning

Some features of the system include:
- Graphical snapshots that include multiple levels of aggregation - including item, location, customer, and/or group, etc.
- Facilitates extended one-number planning and collaboration across the enterprise.
- Multidimensional analysis capabilities
- Promotions, seasonality and organizational strategies incorporated into forecasts
- Pre-trained neural-network models in Event Planning can help analyze potential effects of multiple promotional elements such as price discounts, coupons, advertising and product placements
- Causal-based forecast models support simulations of alternative marketing programs

MANUGISTICS GROUP, INC.
2115 East Jefferson Street
Rockville MD 20852-4905

Software Name: NetWORKS
Phone: 301 984-5000
www.manugistics.com

Commentary: According to Manugistics, NetWORKS™ is an objective, statistical, extrapolative forecasting system that uses multiple methods and a best-fit selection process. As in the case of other "best-fit" forecasting systems, NetWORKS™ selects the forecasting algorithm that best suits the client business. However an additional feature (the "AutoTuner") automatically determines optimal parameter settings. NetWORKS™ also includes advanced causal modeling.

Manugistics has a long history of providing forecasting software to business. In one of its early systems, the company developed a Fourier analysis function for forecasting. In more recent years, the forecasting method used by Manugistics NetWORKS™ has been Lewandowski's Forsys, a modified Holt-Winters approach that incorporates trend dampening.

NetWORKS Demand provides intelligent event modeling capabilities and allows for management overrides. It can links product mix, promotion, and price analyses with traditional demand forecasting, and it enables the simultaneous tracking and understanding of demand along multiple dimensions such as sales, marketing, and logistics.

Some features of the system include:
- Multi-model framework
- Advanced causal modeling
- Event management
- Life cycle forecasting
- Cannibalization modeling

MCCONNELL CHASE SOFTWARE WORKS
360 East Randolph Street, Suite 3202
Chicago IL 60601

Software Name: Forecasting for Demand
Phone: 312 540 1508
www.mcconnellchase.com

Commentary: Forecasting for Demand 6.0 (FD6) is an objective, statistical, extrapolative forecasting system that uses multiple methods and a best-fit selection process. Users can choose between forecasting techniques developed by McConnell Chase and ones that are part of Forecast Pro, licensed from Business Forecast Systems, Inc. Forecast Pro recently outperformed all other software approaches and 18 out of 19 academic teams in the Makridakis-3 study, the largest and most comprehensive empirical forecasting study ever performed.

The system supports level, trend, seasonality, events and other causal modeling, and utilizes a variety of techniques. Among the many methods FD6 provides for generating statistical forecasts are methods for intermittent or low volume items, and methods with non-normal distributions: Poisson, binomial, negative binomial.

FD6 allows for conditioning outliers, providing multiple demand sources (EDI, POS, etc), normalizing irregular periods, optimizing accuracy at specific time periods, data limiting, and substitution/obsolescence linking.
Specifically, the methods include:

- Exponential smoothing
- Double exponential smoothing
- Holt
- Winters
- Box-Jenkins
- Curve fitting,
- Linear and Multiple Regression
- Quadratic curve fitting
- Exponential curve fitting
- Growth curve fitting
- Croston's
- Simple moving average
- Fixed moving average
- Random walk.

FD6 provides a comprehensive and efficient process for factoring in all information on what sales are expected to be. This process combines: Statistical forecasting, which extrapolates the future based on the past, Sales force forecasting, which calibrates and imports the sales funnel and other customer and prospect intelligence, and other customer intelligence, judgement, and management input.

To facilitate collaboration, FD6 provides a comprehensive pivot table, plus extensive graphical and reporting functions, that allow people from every department to aggregate, slice and dice, evaluate, and participate in the forecasting process according to the units and levels of detail in which they think, plan and work. The software also includes forecasting/ planning hierarchies to provide both aggregate and detail control from different perspectives.

PRESCIENT SYSTEMS
1247 Ward Avenue, Suite 200
West Chester, PA 19380

Software Name: Sales Forecasting and Demand Planning
Toll Free: 888-610-1800
www.prescientsystems.com

Commentary: Prescient's Sales Forecasting and Demand Planning modules include an objective, statistical, extrapolative forecasting system that uses multiple methods and a best-fit selection process. Key features include:
- Variable time periods for forecasting in weekly and monthly increments with daily indexing of demand
- Flexible aggregations (pyramids) of demand that model business processes at the product, division, location, customer or other levels
- Support for top-down, bottom-up and middle-out forecasting
- Multiple historical and future demand streams, such as promotions, returns, actual orders, shipments and POS
- New product introduction functionality that creates forecasts for new products by relating historical demand, in whole or in part, from like product(s) to new products

- User-defined record set configuration, facilitating custom presentation of items that meet a specific criteria or are in need of greatest attention
- Extensive simulation capability, enabling users to test the impacts of forecast overrides before applying them
- "Scratchpad" functionality that allows users to compare a variety of data in a dynamic, graphical presentation
- Configurable user interface, which can address a range of needs, from casual to power users, offering tabular and interactive graphical presentation of data
- Data import and export capabilities for integration with a variety of popular systems
- User defined aggregation by total customer, category, product or other groupings
- Configurable alert function to draw user's attention to those items most in need, such as high velocity or slow moving products
- Ability to view and change forecasts in weekly, monthly, quarterly and yearly period
- Evaluates year-to-year growth, sales forecast versus history, sales forecast versus quota, and other user-defined scenarios
- Provides side-by-side comparison of history to forecast, current headquarters' forecast, promotion plans, sales to date along with ability to input new projections or changes
- Flexible user interface personalized to the needs of the user
- Ability to integrate with promotion and trade management applications for a single view of the annual sales plan

SAS

100 SAS Campus Drive
Cary, NC 27513-2414

Phone: (919) 677-8000
www.sas.com

Commentary: SAS provides a set of functions for developing a complete forecasting and demand planning system as well as a pre-configured objective, statistical, extrapolative forecasting system that uses multiple methods and a best-fit selection process.
Contact the company for details on their forecasting software.

SMART SOFTWARE

Four Hill Road
Belmont, MA 02478

Software Name: SmartForecasts
Phone: 800 762-7899
www.smartcorp.com

Commentary: SmartForecasts is an objective, statistical, extrapolative forecasting system that uses multiple methods and a best-fit selection process. The system comes in three different versions SmartForecasts Professional to automatically forecast up to 150 product or other items at a time, SmartForecasts Commercial to forecast up to 1,000 items at a time, and SmartForecasts Enterprise to forecasts up to 100,000 items per hour.

Features of the system include:
- Intuitive Windows User Interface.
- Multiple Windows Displays to view product data, forecast graphs and reports simultaneously.
- Integration with Microsoft Excel. SmartForecasts features an Excel-like spreadsheet interface; full Excel 97/2000 file compatibility; and Cut, Copy and Paste capabilities to transfer forecast data, reports and graphs to other Windows applications.

Context-sensitive On-line Help.

- Best-fit logic incorporates trends, seasonal patterns and the effects of promotions and other special events.
- Interactive Adjustments permit direct adjustment of forecast numbers.
- Multilevel (Multiseries) Forecasting supports top-down and bottom-up forecasts, by product group/item or item/region, for large groups containing hundreds or thousands of items.
- Expanded Promotion and Event Models automatically forecast promotion-driven sales and demand and now allow for different promotional scenarios for each different stockkeeping unit .
- Multivariate Regression for Cause-and-Effect Forecasts.
- Complete Set of Data Analysis Tools include timeplots, scatterplots, auto/cross-correlation analysis, descriptive statistics, seasonal adjustment and time series decomposition.
- Forecast Audit Reports and accuracy measures.
- Automatic Trend Hedging™
- Intermittent Demand Forecasting (patent-pending).
- Import and export data stored in all Excel, Lotus and ASCII file formats, Copy and Paste data from other applications, or transfer data directly from a client/server database system.
- SmartForecasts' Data Table is also multidimensional, accommodating multiple columns for product labels and multiple labels for each item. "Slice and dice" and forecast product data defined by multidimensional criteria (e.g., product item by group, item by region, etc.).

SUPPLY CHAIN CONSULTANTS

5460 Fairmont Drive
Wilmington DE 19808

Phone: 302 738-9215
www.supplychain.com

Commentary: Contact the company for details on their forecasting software.

Appendix D

USE OF EXCEL AND PIVOT TABLES

By

Maurice Seeger
The Dow Chemical Company

Some companies have found that managing data has become a lot easier with the advent of Excel Pivot Tables. The purpose of this appendix is to introduce you to this powerful aspect, Pivot Tables, of Excel.

Definition

A Pivot Table is an interactive table that rapidly summarizes or cross-tabulates large amounts of data. It can rotate rows and columns to see different summaries of source data, filter the data by displaying different pages, or display the details for areas of interest. This allows casual users to become highly competent and independent in their ability to manage and manipulate data quickly and easily.

Building a Pivot Table

In order to use the Pivot Table feature in Excel, you must have a list of data arranged in rows and columns with each column having a unique name in the first row. Typically, the source of data stored within Pivot Tables comes from a data warehouse of some sort - perhaps a forecasting system or an Enterprise Software suite.

Using Pivot Tables

Once an Excel spreadsheet is populated as stated above, manipulating that data is done by simply clicking on the "Pivot Table report . . . ," found under the "Data" menu of Excel. It provides a four-step "wizard" that is easy to use, supported by on-line help buttons. In this manner, a newly formatted spreadsheet is created in accordance with the user's choices. It can be stored in the same spreadsheet folder as the original data source, under a new tab.

While the use of Pivot Tables is somewhat explicit, there are many sources for additional training. Beware, however, because some of the standard publicly offered Excel training classes don't cover the use of Pivot Tables.

Setting up Excel Folders

Often times, separate folders are set up for different functional areas. For example: one folder for forecasting and demand management, and another for production and Rough Cut Capacity Planning. In each of these folders, there are separate tabs for the tabular data and other tabs for the graphical display of that tabular data. The graphical displays are, of course, used in support of discussion and exploration of business issues.

These tabs (both data and graphs) are automatically made current during the routine (daily, weekly, monthly) updating of the data extract from the data warehouse. Additionally, through macros, the folders often are connected and tied together for continuity purposes.

Trend Lines and Patterns

Once a data set has been graphed, Excel offers a variety of trend lines that can be extended backward or forward. Among the options are:

1. Linear
2. Polynomial
3. Logarithmic
4. Exponential
5. Power
6. Moving Average

These are all explained in detail through the help buttons with text and formulas. They can also be customized in a number of ways. This trend line feature is accessed by clicking on a graph and then going to the "Trendline . . ." tab under the "Chart" menu. Additionally, these trend lines can be converted to data values in the table from which the data for the graph came.

One obvious use of these trend lines is to aid in the forecasting process. They are easy to use, explicit, and readily available. They often reduce the need for expensive and complex software for those who are just getting started.

Appendix E

FINISHED GOODS KANBAN

When the demand for an end item (finished product) is repetitive, developing and maintaining a forecast for that item might not be the best way to handle its replenishment.

A simple visual Kanban[1] mechanism may suffice, whereby the item is finished from available materials and components when the finished goods level is diminished to a predetermined amount. Keep in mind that a Kanban mechanism does not plan capacity or materials; it only triggers replenishment. Therefore, the prerequisites for setting up a finished goods Kanban in lieu of a forecast are as follows:

1. The demand is repetitive

2. The materials and components are immediately available, by either
   * Short supplier and component manufacturing lead times
   * Planning bills of material (see Chapter 5)

3. Time to finish the product is relatively short

4. The volume planning is done effectively by another means

This conforms to some of the concepts that those of us who live in North America have learned from the Japanese: "Less is more" and "Simpler is better."

---

[1] A Japanese term which, loosely translated, means sign or signal or trigger.

Appendix F

FORECASTING EFFECTIVENESS CHECKLIST

This checklist is designed to help evaluate how well the forecasting process is being done within a company. As you can readily see, it is built around the forecasting principles we've covered throughout the book.

The approach here is to rate the company's status using YES (we're doing that well), PARTIAL (we're doing some of that but not as well as we should), or NO (we're not doing that and we should be). The first item is a bit of a "gimme."

The intent when using this should be to improve the forecasting process. This is accomplished by turning the NOs and PARTIALs into YESs.

Principle #1: Sales forecasting is being done in virtually every company that produces and sells products, either formally or by default. The challenge is to do it well, better than the competition.

Checklist Item A: Sales forecasting is being done.   **YES PART NO**

Principle #2: Better forecasts enable companies
to give higher customer service (order fill), to lower
the inventories, to run the plants better, to work
more cooperatively with suppliers, and — last but
certainly not least — to sell more product.

**Checklist Item B: These benefits from better forecasting
are widely understood and accepted by key people in   YES PART NO
Sales & Marketing, Operations, and Finance.**

Principle #3: Sales & Marketing people own the sales
forecast; they are accountable for its development,
authorization, and execution.

Checklist Item C: Sales & Marketing have accepted responsibility for forecasting.   YES PART NO

Principle #4: The forecast can and must make sense based on the big picture: economic outlook, industry trends, market share, and so on.

Checklist Item D: The forecasting cycle includes a formal step to relate the newly developed forecast to the economy, the industry, and market share expectations.   YES PART NO

Principle #5: Better processes yield better results; better forecasting processes yield better forecasts.

Checklist Item E: There are multiple inputs to the forecast, not merely history.   YES PART NO

Checklist Item F: Forecasting occurs on a monthly cycle, or possibly more frequently where appropriate.   YES PART NO

Checklist Item G: Most of the forecast is expressed in monthly time periods; in the near future the forecast may be weekly; out beyond one year it may be quarterly.   YES PART NO

Principle #6: The best way to increase forecast accuracy is to focus on reducing forecast error.

Checklist Item H: Forecast error is routinely measured and efforts are made to reduce it. Progress in reducing forecast error is considered more important than the actual amount of error.   YES PART NO

Principle #7: Bias is the worst kind of forecast error; strive for zero bias.

Checklist Item I: Bias in the forecast is routinely measured with the goal of reducing it to zero. Efforts are made to discover the root causes of bias and to eliminate them.
YES   PART   NO

Principle #8: Forecast the volume; manage the mix. Wherever possible, forecast at higher, aggregate levels. Forecast in detail only where necessary.

Checklist Item J: The aggregate forecast is considered the primary forecast, and the detailed forecast is used inside the Planning Time Fence and elsewhere as required. The sum of the detail must equal the aggregate.
YES   PART   NO

Principle #9. One forecast, many views. Have only one forecast, with the ability to display it in a variety of ways for different uses.

Checklist Item K: One and only one forecast, authorized by management, is used throughout the company.
YES   PART   NO

Principle #10: As soon as possible, replace the unknown with the known.

Checklist Item L: Quotes, customer commitments, and customer orders are formally recognized and used as soon as they're known. Effective forecast consumption techniques are routinely used to replace the forecast.
YES   PART   NO

Principle #11: There is far more to be gained by people collaborating and communicating well than by all of the advanced formulas and algorithms yet developed.

Checklist Item M: Teamwork and good communication processes are widely recognized as the key to better forecasts. Complaining, whining, and finger pointing are not considered appropriate and are discouraged.
YES   PART   NO

Principle #12: Better processes yield better results;
better production, purchasing, and scheduling processes
help to get better forecasts.

**Checklist Item #N: Operations people recognize their
role in improving the forecasts, and are actively engaged in**   **YES PART NO**
**efforts to reduce lead times and improve other aspects of
the production, purchasing, and scheduling processes.**

A company that can answer YES to all 14 of the checklist items can be virtually certain that its forecasting processes are working well. Twelve or 13 YESs are very good.

Please remember: the purpose here is to make things better. Use this checklist as a guide for improvement.

Appendix G

Sample Forecasting Displays

The following is a series of very simplified and scaled down displays used in the forecasting process. Our purpose here is not to provide specifics on report and screen formats, but rather to give the reader a sense of how the numbers might look at the various stages in the development of the forecast. (In actual practice, forecasting displays tend to be somewhat intimidating at first glance, because they contain lots of numbers.)

We start with a product family: large industrial widgets.

FAMILY: LARGE INDUST'L WIDGETS	A	M	J	J	A	S	O	N	D	J	F	M	TOT	MOS 13-15	MOS 16-18
LAST 12 MONTHS ACTUAL	91	86	90	93	88	92	95	93	83	100	101	98	1110		
NEXT 18 MONTHS FORECAST: SYSTEM	100	100	100	100	100	100	100	100	100	100	100	100	1200	300	300
MGMT															

We can see several things:

- This forecast is for a family: large industrial widgets. As such, it is a forecast of overall volume, not mix.

- The forecast interval is monthly, which is appropriate for volume forecasts.

- The horizon extends 18 months into the future, which also is appropriate for volume.

- This year's forecast of 1,200 units is about ten percent higher than last year's actual.

- This is a (forecasting) system-generated forecast. No management override has yet been entered.

Next we see the results of adding the mix detail to the picture.

FAMILY: LARGE INDUST'L WIDGETS	A	M	J	J	A	S	O	N	D	J	F	M	TOT	MOS 13-15	MOS 16-18
LAST 12 MONTHS ACTUAL	91	86	90	93	88	92	95	93	83	100	101	98	1110		
NEXT 18 MONTHS FORECAST: SYSTEM	100	100	100	100	100	100	100	100	100	100	100	100	1200	300	300
MGMT															
WIDGET L1 FORECAST: SYSTEM	60	60	60												
MGMT															
WIDGET L2 FORECAST: SYSTEM	30	30	30												
MGMT															
WIDGET L3 FORECAST: SYSTEM	10	10	10												
MGMT															
TOTAL INDIVIDUAL PRODUCTS SYSTEM	100	100	100												
MGMT															

◄— **Planning Time Fence**

Several points are important here:

- The mix detail has been added, showing forecasts for individual products L1, L2, and L3.

- The horizon for this detail is three months. This is the cumulative procurement and production lead time for large industrial widgets, and thus the Planning Time Fence is set at this point.

- The sum of the individual forecasts equals the family, volume forecast.

Next we see the addition of feedback from the field sales people. Because these are the folks "on the ground" with customers every day, most companies value their input highly, particularly inside the Planning Time Fence, which of course is where the detailed, mix forecast often comes into play. In the next display, the sales manager has accepted the input from the field for inclusion into the forecast.

FAMILY: LARGE INDUST'L WIDGETS	A	M	J	J	A	S	O	N	D	J	F	M	T O T	MOS 13-15	MOS 16-18
LAST 12 MONTHS ACTUAL	91	86	90	93	88	92	95	93	83	100	101	98	1110		
NEXT 18 MONTHS FORECAST: SYSTEM	100	100	100	100	100	100	100	100	100	100	100	100	1200	300	300
MGMT															
WIDGET L1 FORECAST: SYSTEM	60	60	60												
MGMT		70	70												
WIDGET L2 FORECAST: SYSTEM	30	30	30												
MGMT			35												
WIDGET L3 FORECAST: SYSTEM	10	10	10												
MGMT															
TOTAL INDIVIDUAL PRODUCTS SYSTEM	100	100	100												
MGMT	100	**110** ********	**115** ********												

◄——— **Planning Time Fence**

Here we see an issue: The sum of the detail does not match the aggregate. What needs to happen next is that the aggregate and the detail must be reconciled. After that is done, the forecast would appear as follows:

FAMILY: LARGE INDUST'L WIDGETS	A	M	J	J	A	S	O	N	D	J	F	M	T O T	MOS 13-15	MOS 16-18
LAST 12 MONTHS ACTUAL	91	86	90	93	88	92	95	93	83	100	101	98	1110		
NEXT 18 MONTHS FORECAST: SYSTEM	100	100	100	100	100	100	100	100	100	100	100	100	1200	300	300
MGMT		110	115										1225		
WIDGET L1 FORECAST: SYSTEM	60	60	60												
MGMT		70	70												
WIDGET L2 FORECAST: SYSTEM	30	30	30												
MGMT			35												
WIDGET L3 FORECAST: SYSTEM	10	10	10												
MGMT															
TOTAL INDIVIDUAL PRODUCTS SYSTEM	100	100	100												
MGMT	100	110	115												

←—— **Planning Time Fence**

Subsequently, the senior Sales & Marketing executives review this forecast prior to its release. They're concerned about a potential volume decline beginning in the fall, for two reasons:

1. They plan to introduce a new medium industrial widget in September, which will have capabilities almost on a par with some of the large models, but will sell for less money. They expect that this new model will cannibalize some volume from the large widget family.

2. The economy is expected to soften during the second half of the calendar year.

For this reason, they elect to lower the forecast, beginning in October. The results of their decision are shown below.

FAMILY: LARGE INDUST'L WIDGETS	A	M	J	J	A	S	O	N	D	J	F	M	TOT	MOS 13-15	MOS 16-18
LAST 12 MONTHS ACTUAL	91	86	90	93	88	92	95	93	83	100	101	98	1110		
NEXT 18 MONTHS FORECAST: SYSTEM	100	100	100	100	100	100	100	100	100	100	100	100	1200	300	300
MGMT		110	115				90	90	90	90	90	90	1165	270	270
WIDGET L1 FORECAST: SYSTEM	60	60	60												
MGMT		70	70												
WIDGET L2 FORECAST: SYSTEM	30	30	30												
MGMT			35												
WIDGET L3 FORECAST: SYSTEM	10	10	10												
MGMT															
TOTAL INDIVIDUAL PRODUCTS SYSTEM	100	100	100												
MGMT	100	110	115												

◀—— **Planning Time Fence**

The assumptions that underlie this forecast should be documented. They might appear as follows:

1. Anticipating higher than normal demand on models L1 and L2 during May-June from Ajax Inc.

2. This family expected to lose volume to new medium widget product beginning in October.

3. Economy forecasted to be soft in second half of year, with attendant drop in housing starts.

Subsequent steps could include dollarizing the new forecasts for this and all other families, and evaluating the potential impact on the business plan. In companies using Sales & Operations Planning, this management-authorized forecast is the primary input into the monthly S&OP cycle, which aims to balance demand and supply and evaluate the impact of forecast changes on the business plan.

Appendix H

Exponential Smoothing Formulas

by

Bill Montgomery, CFPIM, CIRM

and the

Orange County, California APICS Chapter

Exponential Smoothing is a weighted moving average technique that is widely used in generating statistical forecasts. Many companies find Exponential Smoothing attractive because it:
- is easy to understand,
- is simple to adjust to changing conditions,
- incorporates trend and seasonal patterns,
- minimizes data storage and calculations.

Exponential Smoothing "smoothes" historical data into the old forecast to calculate the new forecast. Its basic formula is, in English:

The new forecast equals the old forecast plus a percentage of the forecast error from the prior period.

Symbolically: $Fn = Fo + \alpha(Da - Fo)$ where Fn = New forecast
Fo = Old forecast (from the period just ended)
α = Alpha (the smoothing factor)
Da = Actual demand (from the period just ended)

Let's take a look. Assume an old forecast of 100, an alpha of 0.1, and actual demanf of 110. Then

$$Fn = 100 + .1(110 - 100)$$
$$= 100 + .1(10)$$
$$= 100 + 1$$
$$= 101$$

What's happened here is that we sold ten more than we forecasted for last month. The formula took a portion of that forecast error (0.1 or 10 percent) and added it into the forecast.

Is ten percent too high or too low? It depends. Let's look at this alpha more closely.

The Smoothing Factor

The smoothing factor, alpha, determines how much recent historical data is entered into the new forecast. A very low alpha, say 0.001, means that the new actual demand would have a relatively minor impact on the forecast. This would result in a forecast that is very stable but not highly responsive. It would be quite slow to change.

A high alpha causes the reverse to happen; the new forecast will be impacted heavily by the latest actual sales. Carrying it to the extreme, an alpha of 1.0 would apply to *all* of the last period's actual demand to the forecast. In other words, the new forecast would be *the same as last period's demand*. This of course would result in a forecast that is highly responsive, but extremely unstable: always "chasing" the most recent demand. Not a good thing.

The formula here is $\alpha = 2/N+1$, where N is the number of periods of actual demand that will influence the forecast. From it, we can conclude that:

An α of **1.0**   will result in   **1** period of demand history in the forecast.
An α of **0.5**   will result in   **3** periods of demand history in the forecast.
An α of **0.33**   will result in   **5** periods of demand history in the forecast.
An α of **0.2**   will result in   **9** periods of demand history in the forecast.
An α of **0.1**   will result in   **19** periods of demand history in the forecast.

The word "exponential" refers to the fact that there is an exponential decay to the weighting of history as it gets older. More weight is given to the more recent periods than those that are older.

An Example

Let's take a product with a forecast of 175 per month. Over time, the actual demand has been 169, 180, 135, 213, 181, 148, and 204. First, we'll look at what would have resulted from an alpha of 0.1. See Figure H-1.

Figure H -1		**Exponential Smoothing Example** **Alpha = 0.1**				
Fn =	**Fo +**	**α**	**Da - Fo**	**Dev**	**αDev**	**Rnd**
174 =	175 +	.1	169 - 175	-6	-0.6	-1
175 =	174 +	.1	180 - 174	6	0.6	1
171 =	175 +	.1	135 - 175	-40	-4.0	-4
175 =	171 +	.1	213 - 171	42	4.2	4
176 =	175 +	.1	181 - 175	6	0.6	1
173 =	176 +	.1	148 - 176	-28	-2.8	-3
176 =	173 +	.1	204 - 173	31	3.1	3

Notice how the forecast remained relatively stable during this period as demand was bouncing around a good bit; the forecasts moved from a low of 171 to a high of 176. In Figure H-2, we can see how the same product would look with an alpha of 0.5.

Figure H -2		**Exponential Smoothing Example** **Alpha = 0.5**				
Fn =	**Fo +**	**α**	**Da - Fo**	**Dev**	**αDev**	**Rnd**
172 =	175 +	.5	169 - 175	-6	-3	-3
176 =	172 +	.5	180 - 172	8	4	4
155 =	176 +	.5	135 - 176	-41	-20.5	-21
184 =	155 +	.5	213 - 155	58	29	29
182 =	184 +	.5	181 - 184	-3	-1.5	-2
165 =	182 +	.5	148 - 182	-34	-17	-17
185 =	165 +	.5	204 - 165	39	20	20

In this example the forecast was much less stable, ranging from a low of 155 in period 3 to a high of 185 in period 7. The forecast was certainly responsive, perhaps to a fault. Many would argue that the variations in demand seen here are merely random variability around a relatively constant mean, and that the best forecasting approach is one that "cuts through the middle" of the ups and downs. Stability and linearity are good; chasing after random variability is not.

Many forecasters feel that the best forecasts contain a balance of stability and responsiveness, and as such they'll tend to use alpha factors in the range of 0.05 to 0.2. There will always be random variations in the forecasts. A primary purpose of the forecasting process is the tracking of performance, the identification of significant variations and bias. Demand filters will identify unusual demand and tracking signals (see p. 44) and can identify unacceptable levels of bias.

Trend

A lower alpha can pose a problem with items whose demand is trending up or down. In this case, the forecasting model needs to be more responsive because the real world is changing rapidly. To deal with this, Exponential Smoothing handles trend items in a different way: It smoothes and updates not only the forecast but also the magnitude of the trend. Here are the formulas, first for updating the forecast:

$$Fn = Fo + \alpha D\ (Da - Fo) + To, \text{ where}$$

Fn	= New forecast
Fo	= Old forecast (from the period just ended)
αD	= Alpha (the smoothing factor for demand)
Da	= Actual demand (from the period just ended)
To	= Old trend

Now let's look at the formula for smoothing the trend:

$$Tn = To + \alpha T\ (Dev - To), \text{ where}$$

Tn	= New trend
To	= Old trend
αT	= Alpha for trend
Dev	= Actual demand – Old forecast (Da – Fo, from the forecast calculation)

Let's see how it works. This item, shown in Figure H-3, has an old forecast of 100 and is trending upward, with an (old) trend calculated at 6. First, look at the top half of the figure and temporarily disregard the lines and arrows. In period 1, we can see that the trend of 6 was added to the old forecast (100) plus the smoothed deviation of 2 (.2 x (110 - 100)), resulting in a new forecast of 108.

Figure H - 3   **TREND CALCULATIONS**

Fn = Fo + α D (Da - Fo) Dev + (αDev + To)

108 = 100 + 0.2 (110 - 100)   10 + (2.0 + 6.0)

113 = 108 + 0.2 (100 - 108)   -8 + (-1.6 + 6.4)

119 = 113 + 0.2 (120 - 113)   7 + (1.4 + 5.0)

126 = 119 + 0.2 (130 - 119)   11 + (2.2 + 5.2)

131 = 126 + 0.2 (120 - 126)   -6 + (-1.2 + 5.8)

137 = 131 + 0.2 (140 - 131)   9 + (1.8 + 4.6)

Tn = To + αT Dev - To) Dev αDev

6.4 = 6.0 + 0.1 (10 - 6.0)   4.0   0.4

5.0 = 6.4 + 0.1 (- 8 - 6.4) -14.4   -1.4

5.2 = 5.0 + 0.1 (..7 - 5.0)   2.0   0.2

5.8 = 5.2 + 0.1 (11 - 5.2)   5.8   0.6

4.6 = 5.8 + 0.1 (-6 - 5.8) -11.8   -1.2

5.0 = 4.6 + 0.1 (9 - 4.6)   4.4   0.4

In the lower half of Figure H-3, we can see the trend being smoothed. In period 1, the Dev of 10 is coming from the calculated deviation at the top of the figure. Similarly, the To (old trend) is brought down from the top formula. The result of 4 is smoothed via the alpha of 0.1 to become 0.4 and updates Tn, the new trend value. In the next period, Tn becomes To and is updated by that period's activity.

An item can get identified as a candidate for trend forecasting in several ways:

- It's a new product and demand is expected to ramp up sharply.

- It's an old product, entering end-of-life, and is expected to decline.

- The forecaster has reason to believe that an existing item is going to "take off" or slow down, perhaps due to pricing, competitive issues, and so forth.

- The item's tracking signal exceeds its tracking signal limit, and the forecasting system so notifies the forecaster, who concludes that the item is in a trend condition. (See page 44).

Seasonal

Seasonal items — sporting goods, lawn care products, and school furniture among many others — require a different forecasting approach. The method used in Exponential Smoothing is to establish a base series (of monthly indexes) which defines the "seasonal curve" of historical demand for the item. In Figure H-4, we can see how the month-by-month index is created.

Figure H-4	ESTABLISHING THE BASE SERIES FOR SEASONAL ADJUSTMENT				
MO	YR-1	YR-2	YR-3	Total	Index
Jan	525	520	460	1505	.120
Feb	400	440	310	1150	.091
Mar	200	300	290	790	.063
Apr	65	70	75	210	.017
May	50	50	50	150	.012
Jun	90	75	85	250	.020
Jul	200	200	150	550	.044
Aug	400	400	390	1190	.095
Sep	550	450	500	1500	.119
Oct	470	450	705	1625	.129
Nov	550	630	495	1675	.133
Dec	700	715	580	1995	.158
Total	4200	4300	4090	12590	1.0

Here we can see, for example, that January demand is 12 percent of annual (.120 in decimal form), while May is at a low of 01.2 percent and December the highest with 15.8 percent of the total year. This item sells mostly in the winter months, and little in spring and early summer.

Next compute the demand ratio, which is the actual demand divided by the index for the month. The formula for this is $R = Da/Index$ where

R	= Demand ratio
Da	= Actual demand
Index	= Base series index for the month

The demand radio is, in effect, the "annualized demand" based on demand for a single month, i.e., the one just ended. Since it's annualized, the seasonality is no longer present.

See Figure H-5, section 1.

Figure H-5

CALCULATING SEASONAL DEMAND

1. COMPUTE DEMAND RATIO

	MO	Da	/	INDEX	= Demand Ratio "R"
A	JAN	600	/	0.120	= 5000
B	FEB	350	/	0.091	= 3846
C	MAR	180	/	0.063	= 2857
D	APR	100	/	0.017	= 5882

2. EXPONENTIALLY SMOOTH DEMAND RATIO "R"

	MO	Rn	=	Ro	+	α	(R - Ro)	DEV	αDEV
A	JAN	4288	=	4209	+	0.1	(5000 - 4209)	791	79
B	FEB	4244	=	4288	+	0.1	(3846 - 4288)	- 442	- 44
C	MAR	4105	=	4244	+	0.1	(2857 - 4244)	-1387	-139
D	APR	4283	=	4105	+	0.1	(5882 - 4105)	1777	178

3. CALCULATE ADJUSTED NEW FORECAST FOR EACH MONTH

	MO	Fn	=	Rn	x	INDEX
A	FEB	390	=	4288	x	0.091
B	MAR	267	=	4244	x	0.063
C	APR	70	=	4105	x	0.017
D	MAY	51	=	4283	x	0.012

Next, exponentially smooth the demand ratio. See Figure H-5, section 2.

Last, calculate the adjusted new forecast for each month by applying the index to the new Rn's. This puts the forecast back into monthly increments and re-applies the seasonality. See section 3 of Figure H-5.

It's possible to have a seasonal item that is trending up or down. Within Exponential Smoothing, there is a technique called trend/seasonal, which in effect, overlays the seasonal curve on top of the trend calculations. This is beyond our scope here, but to pursue it, you can check John Mentzer and Carol Bienstock's book, *Sales Forecasting Management*, referenced in the Bibliography on page 163.

Glossary

Author's note: Wherever practical, we've tried to use existing definitions from the ninth edition of the APICS Dictionary [2]. Those have been noted (APICS). The definitions we have supplied ourselves are in italics.

Abnormal Demand — *Large demand not in the forecast, frequently from a customer with whom the company has not been doing business.*

Accessory — *A product that has benefit when used in conjunction with another product. For example, a docking station for a laptop computer is an accessory. Not to be confused with option; an automatic transmission for a car is an option. See:* **Supply Item.**

Aggregate Forecast — *See:* **Volume Forecast.**

Assemble-to-Order — A production environment where a good or service can be assembled after receipt of a customer's order. The key components (bulk, semifinished, intermediate, subassembly, fabricated, purchased, packaging, etc.) used in the assembly or finishing process are planned and possibly stocked in anticipation of a customer order. Receipt of an order initiates assembly of the customized product. This strategy is useful where a large number of end products (based on the selection of options and accessories) can be assembled from common components. (APICS)

Available-to-Promise — *That portion of an item's inventory and scheduled production not yet committed to customer orders or other firm demands.*

Bias — *The amount of forecast error build-up over time, plus or minus. This is a measure of over-forecasting or under-forecasting. See:* **Running Sum of Forecast Error.**

Blow-down — *The act of deriving detailed, mix forecasts from the aggregate, volume forecast. See:* **Roll-up.**

Build-to-Order — *Term popularized by Dell Computer which means much the same thing as* **Assemble-to-Order.**

---

[2] James F. Cox III and John H. Blackstone Jr., eds., *APICS Dictionary, ninth edition* (Falls Church, Virginia: APICS, 1998). Terms and definitions used with permission.

Business Plan — 1) A statement of long-range strategy and revenue, cost, and profit objectives usually accompanied by budgets, a projected balance sheet, and a cash flow (source and application of funds) statement. A business plan is usually stated in terms of dollars and grouped by product family. The business plan, the sales and operations plan, and the production plan, although frequently stated in different terms, should agree with each other. . . . 2) A document consisting of the business details (organization, strategy, financing tactics) prepared by an entrepreneur to plan for a new business. (APICS)

Capacity Planning — *The process of determining how much capacity will be required to produce in the future. Capacity planning can occur at an aggregate level (see* **Rough-cut Capacity Planning**) *or at a detailed level. Tools employed for the latter include the traditional Capacity Requirements Planning process and the newer Finite Capacity Planning/Scheduling, which not only recognize specific overloads but make recommendations for overcoming them.*

Critical Time Fence — *See:* **Planning Time Fence.**

Demand Management — The function of recognizing all demands for goods and services to support the marketplace. It involves doing what is required to help make the demand happen and prioritizing demand when supply is lacking. Proper demand management facilitates the planning and use of resources for profitable business results. It encompasses the activities of forecasting, order entry, order promising, and determining branch warehouse requirements, interplant orders, and service parts requirements. (APICS)

Demand Manager — *A job function charged with coordinating the demand management process. Frequently the demand manager will operate the statistical forecasting system and work closely with other marketing and salespeople in the Demand Planning phase of S&OP. Other activities for the demand manager might include making decisions regarding abnormal demand, working closely with the master scheduler on product availability issues, and being a key player in other aspects of the monthly Sales & Operations Planning process. This may or may not be a full-time position.*

Demand Plan — *The forecast, customer orders, and other anticipated demands such as interplant, export, and samples. See:* **Sales Plan.**

Detailed Forecast — *See:* **Mix Forecast.**

End Item — *An individual finished product. See:* **Stockkeeping Unit.**

Enterprise Resources Planning (ERP) System — 1) An accounting-oriented information system for identifying and planning the enterprise-wide resources needed to take, make, ship, and account for customer orders. An ERP system differs from the typical MRP II system in technical requirements such as graphical user interface, relational database, use of fourth-generation language, and computer-assisted software engineering tools in development, client/server architecture, and open-system portability. 2) More generally, a method for the effective planning and control of all resources needed to take, make, ship, and account for customer orders in a manufacturing, distribution, or service company. (APICS)

Executive S&OP Meeting — *The culminating step in the monthly Sales & Operations Planning cycle. It is a decision-making meeting, attended by the president/general manager, his or her staff, and other key individuals.*

Family — *See:* **Product Family.**

Financial Interface — *A process of tying financial information and operating information together. It is the process by which businesses are able to operate with one and only one set of numbers, rather than using data in operational functions that differ from that used in the financial side of the business.*

Financial Planning — *The process of developing dollarized projections for revenues, costs, cash flow, other asset changes, and so forth.*

Finish-to-Order — *See:* **Assemble-to-Order.**

Forecast — *See:* **Sales Forecast**

Forecast Error — *The amount that the forecast deviates from actual sales. Measures of forecast error include* **Mean Absolute Deviation** *(MAD) and* **Sum of Deviations** *(SOD).* *See:* **Variability.**

Forecast Frequency — *How often the forecast is fully reviewed and updated. A monthly frequency is common.*

Forecast Horizon — *The amount of time into the future that the forecast covers.*

Forecast Interval — *The size or "width" of the time period being forecasted. The most commonly used intervals are weekly or monthly.*

Make-to-Order — A production environment where a good or service can be made after receipt of a customer's order. The final product is usually a combination of standard items and items custom-designed to meet the special needs of the customer. Where options or accessories are stocked before customer orders arrive, the term assemble-to-order is frequently used. See: Assemble-to-Order, Make-to-Stock. (APICS)

Make-to-Stock — A production environment where products can be and usually are finished before receipt of a customer order. Customer orders are typically filled from existing stocks, and production orders are used to replenish those stocks. See: **Assemble-to-Order, Make-to-Order.** (APICS)

Manufacturing Resource Planning (MRP II) — A method for the effective planning of all resources of a manufacturing company. Ideally, it addresses operational planning in units, financial planning in dollars, and has a simulation capability to answer "what if" questions. It is made up of a variety of functions, each linked together: business planning, sales and operations planning, production planning, master production scheduling, material requirements planning, capacity requirements planning, and the execution support systems for capacity and material. Output from these systems is integrated with financial reports such as the business plan, purchase commitment report, shipping budget, and inventory projections in dollars.... (APICS)

Master Production Schedule (MPS) — 1) The anticipated build schedule for those items assigned to the master scheduler. The master scheduler maintains this schedule, and in turn, it becomes a set of planning numbers that drives material requirements planning. It represents what the company plans to produce expressed in specific configurations, quantities, and dates. The master production schedule is not a sales forecast that represents a statement of demand. The master production schedule must take into account the forecast, the production plan, and other important considerations such as backlog, availability of material, availability of capacity, and management policies and goals. Syn: **master schedule.** 2) The result of the master scheduling process. The master schedule is a presentation of demand, forecast, backlog, the MPS, the projected on-hand inventory, and the available-to-promise quantity. (APICS)

Master Schedule — *See:* **Master Production Schedule.**

Mean Absolute Deviation (MAD) — *A measure of forecast error. It refers to the amount that actual demand deviates from the mean (the forecast) on an absolute basis, i.e. irrespective of whether the error is plus or minus.*

Mix — *The details. Individual products, customer orders, pieces of equipment — as opposed to aggregate groupings. See:* **Volume.**

Mix Forecast — *A forecast by individual products. Sometimes called the detailed forecast. It is used for short-term scheduling for plants and suppliers, (and may be required for certain long lead time, unique purchased items).*

Operations Plan — *The agreed-upon rates and volumes of production or procurement to support the Sales Plan (Demand Plan, Sales Forecast) and to reach the inventory or order backlog targets. The Operations Plan, upon authorization at the Executive S&OP meeting, becomes the "marching orders" for the master scheduler, who must set the Master Production Schedule in congruence with the Operations Plan.*

Order Fill Rate — *The percentage of customer orders shipped on time and complete as opposed to the total number of orders. Order fill is a more stringent measure of customer delivery performance than line fill. For example, if only one item out of twenty on a customer order is unavailable, then that order counts for zero in the order fill calculation. The line fill percentage in this example would be 95 percent. See:* **Line Fill Rate.**

Planning Bill of Material — An artificial grouping of items or events in bill-of-material format used to facilitate master scheduling and material planning. (APICS)

Planning Time Fence — *the time frame inside of which detailed planning must be present in the Master Schedule. Sometimes called the Critical Time Fence. See Appendix A in this book.*

Pre-SOP Meeting — *The preliminary session prior to the Executive S&OP meeting. In it, key people from Sales and Marketing, Operations, Finance, and New Product Development come together to develop the recommendations to be made at the Executive S&OP session.*

Product Family — *The basic planning element for Sales & Operations Planning. S&OP's focus is on families and subfamilies (volume), not individual items (mix).*

Product Subfamily — *A planning element sometimes used in S&OP that provides a more detailed view than product families, but not at the extreme detail of individual products. Product Family A, for example, might contain three subfamilies — A1, A2, A3 — and each of those might contain a dozen or so individual products. See:* **Product Family.**

Production Plan — *See:* **Operations Plan.**

Resource — Anything that adds value to a good or service in its creation, production, or delivery. (APICS)

Resource Requirements Planning — *See:* **Rough-Cut Capacity Planning.**

RFSE — *See:* **Running Sum of Forecast Error**

Roll-up — *The act of creating an aggregate, volume forecast by summing up the detailed, mix forecasts. See:* **Blow-down.**

Rough-Cut Capacity Planning — *The process by which the Operations Plan or the Master Production Schedule can be converted into future capacity requirements. Frequently the Operations Plan, expressed in units of product, is "translated" into standard hours of workload (which is a common unit of measure for production operations). Rough-Cut Capacity Planning can be used at the departmental level, or for subsets of departments down to individual pieces of equipment or specific skill levels for production associates. This process can also be carried out for suppliers, for warehouse space, and for non-production operations such as product design and drafting.*

Running Sum of Forecast Error (RFSE) — *The cumulative sum of forecast error, plus or minus, over time. As such, it is a measure of bias. Also called Sum of Deviations (SOD).*

Sales & Operations Planning (S&OP) — *A business process that helps companies keep demand and supply in balance. It does that by focusing on aggregate volumes - product families and groups - so that mix issues - individual products and customer orders - can be handled more readily. It occurs on a monthly cycle and displays information in both units and dollars. S&OP is cross-functional, involving General Management, Sales, Operations, Finance, and Product Development. It occurs at multiple levels within the company, up to and including the executive in charge of the business unit, e.g,. division president, business unit general manager, or CEO of a smaller corporation. S&OP links the company's Strategic Plans and Business Plan to its detailed processes - the order entry, master scheduling, plant scheduling, and purchasing tools it uses to run the business on a week-to-week, day-to-day, and hour-to-hour basis. Used properly, S&OP enables the company's managers to view the business holistically and provides them with a window into the future.*

Sales Forecast — *A projection of estimated future demand.*

Sales Plan — A time-phased statement of expected customer orders anticipated to be received ... for each major product family or item. It represents sales and marketing management's commitment to take all reasonable steps necessary to achieve this level of actual customer orders. The Sales Plan is a necessary input to the ... sales and operations planning process.... (APICS)

Service Part — *An item used in the repair or maintenance of equipment. Also called spares or repair parts.*

Stockkeeping Unit (SKU) — *An individual finished product. In the more rigorous use of the term, it refers to a specific, individual product in a given location. Thus, product #1234 at the Los Angeles warehouse is a different SKU from the same product at the Chicago warehouse. See:* **End Item.**

Subfamily — *See:* **Product Subfamily.**

Sum of Deviations (SOD) — *See:* **Running Sum of Forecast Error.**

Supply Chain — 1) The processes from the initial raw materials to the ultimate consumption of the finished product linking across supplier-user companies. 2) The functions inside and outside a company that enable the value chain to make products and provide services to the customer. (APICS)

Supply Chain Management — The planning, organizing, and controlling of supply chain activities. (APICS)

Supply Item — *An item that is consumed in the operation of a product. Printer cartridges are supply items. See:* **Accessory.**

Supply Planning — *The function of setting planned rates of production (both in-house and outsourced) to satisfy the Demand Plan and to meet inventory and order backlog targets. Frequently, Rough-cut Capacity Planning is used to support this.*

Time Fence — A policy or guideline established to note where various restrictions or changes in operating procedures take place. For example, changes to the master production scheduled can be accomplished easily beyond the cumulative lead time while changes inside the cumulative lead time become increasingly more difficult to a point where changes should be resisted. Time fences can be used to define these points.(APICS)

Variability — *In the larger sense, this is the amount that individual elements in a time series deviate from the average. In some cases, variability is random and inherent in the process being observed. In this book, we used variability to mean the average forecast error per period. See:* **Forecast Error.**

Volume — *The big picture. Sales and production rates for aggregate groupings — product families, production departments, etc. — as opposed to individual products, customer orders, and work centers. See:* **Mix.**

Volume Forecast — *A forecast by product groupings such as families, classes, and so forth. Also called the aggregate forecast or the product gronup forecast, it is used for sales planning, for capacity planning at the plants and suppliers, and for financial analysis and projections.*

BIBLIOGRAPHY

Books

Clement, Jerry, Andy Coldrick, & John Sari. *Manufacturing Data Structures-Building Foundations for Excellence with Bills of Materials & Process Information.* New York: John Wiley & Sons, 1992.

Colt, Stockton B., Jr., & Towers Perrin. *The Sales Compensation Handbook.* New York: American Management Association, 1998.

Davenport, Thomas H. *Mission Critical-Realizing the Promise of Enterprise System.* Boston, MA: Harvard Business School Press, 2000.

Goldman, Steven L., Roger N. Nagel, & Kenneth Preiss. *Agile Competitors and Virtual Organizations — Strategies for Enriching the Customer.* New York: Van Nostrand Reinhold, Inc., 1995.

Mentzer, John T., & Carol C. Bienstock. *Sales Forecasting Management.* Thousand Oaks, California: Sage Publications, Inc., 1998.

Palmatier, George E., & Joseph S. Shull. *The Marketing Edge-The New Leadership Role of Sales & Marketing in Manufacturing.* New York: John Wiley & Sons, 1989.

Proud, John F. *Master Scheduling-A Practical Guide to Competitive Manufacturing, Second Edition.* New York: John Wiley & Sons, 1999.

Sandras, Jr., William A. *Just-In-Time: Making It Happen-Unleashing the Power of Continuous Improvement.* New York: John Wiley & Sons, 1989.

Shigeo, Shingo. *A Revolution in Manufacturing: The SMED System.* Portland, OR: Productivity Press, 1985.

Smith, Bernard T. *Focus Forecasting-Computer Techniques for Inventory Control.* Boston, MA: CBI Publishing, 1978.

Wallace, Thomas F. *Sales & Operations Planning: The How-To Handbook.* Cincinnati, OH: T.F. Wallace & Company, 1999.

Wallace, Thomas F. & Michael H. Kremzar. *ERP: Making It Happen — The Implementers' Guide to Success with Enterprise Resource Planning.* New York: John Wiley & Sons, 2001.

Womack, James P., & Daniel T. Jones. *Lean Thinking: Banish Waste & Create Wealth in Your Corporation.* NY: Schuster, 1996.

Booklets

Brassard, Michael, (Ed.). *The Memory Jogger — A Pocket Guide of Tools for Continuous Improvement.* Methuen, MA: GOAL/QPC, 1998.

Edelman, Martin P., (Ed.). *Practical Forecasting.* Falls Church, VA: APICS Training Aid, 1985.

Articles

Johnson, George. "Dear APICS." *APICS — The Performance Advantage,* April 1999, (p. 22).

Latamore, Bert. "An Interview with John M. Paterson, VP & Chief Procurement Officer, IBM." *APICS — The Performance Advantage,* October 2000, (pp. 33-35).

Smart, Charles, & Thomas Willemain, Ph.D., "Get Real — A New Way to Forecast Intermittent Demand." *APICS — The Performance Advantage,* June 2000, (pp. 64-68).

Wallace, Thomas F. "Forecasting 101." *APICS — The Performance Advantage,* March 1996, (pp. 80-81).

Wallace, Thomas F. "Stamp Out Forecast Accuracy: How the Push for Super-Accurate Forecasts Can Be Counterproductive." *APICS — The Performance Advantage,* April 1999, (pp. 68-69).

Papers

Swan, Lorne. "Forecasting Methods." St. Louis, MO: Demand Strategies Group, Inc. 2000.

Garwood, R. Dave, & Darryl Landvater. "The New Thinking on Sales Forecasting," APICS Conference Proceedings, October 1985, (pp.729-730).

Index

SCOTT FORESMAN · ADDISON WESLEY

Mathematics

Grade K

Every Student Learns

With a Foreword by Dr. Jim Cummins

ESL Consultant
Darrel Nickolaisen
Teacher/Consultant
Apple Valley, California

Editorial Offices: Glenview, Illinois • Parsippany, New Jersey • New York, New York

Sales Offices: Parsippany, New Jersey • Duluth, Georgia • Glenview, Illinois
Coppell, Texas • Ontario, California • Mesa, Arizona

Overview

Every Student Learns is a lesson-by-lesson companion to
Scott Foresman - Addison Wesley Mathematics and Matemáticas Scott
Foresman - Addison Wesley. It has been designed to provide manageable
support for teachers and their students who are challenged by language issues in
Mathematics, no matter what the first language may be.

Every Student Learns is built upon the Three Pillars of English Language Learning
in the Content Areas by Dr. Jim Cummins of the University of Toronto:

• Activate Prior Knowledge/Build Background

• Access Content

• Extend Language

ISBN: 0-328-07549-3

5 6 7 8 9 10 V004 09 08 07 06 05